Love and Luck

A Young Woman's Journey

from Berlin to Shanghai

to San Francisco

Karen Levi

Opus Press | Washington, D.C. | 2016

Printed on Opus, an Espresso Book Machine located at:
Politics and Prose Bookstore
5015 Connecticut Ave NW
Washington, D.C. 20008

Love and Luck

To my siblings
Constance Rose and Laurence Alfons Karl
a.k.a. Connie and Larry

Introduction

"Everybody has a story to tell. The trouble is these days people don't believe their stories are worth much. But we have to tell our stories; otherwise, how are we going to know who we are? We have to listen to the stories of other people; how else are we going to know who they are?"
- Steven Kent

My mother, Eva Wolffheim Levi, has a guardian angel watching over her. She has been blessed with long life, health, and a youthful appearance that defies the imagination. She was born in Berlin, Germany in 1927 to Jewish parents, part of a large extended family of long-time Berliners; upper middle-class people who thrived in the cosmopolitan cultural life of the city. I heard once that the secret of life is love and luck. Of course there is a good deal more, but my mother has these two gifts in abundance, along with a fierce determination to enjoy life, never-ending optimism and a sense of humor. In my observation of her, Eva has few fears. Maybe these aspects of my mother explain why I have always liked the children's book, *Madeline*, and the specific lines, "She was not afraid of mice, winter, snow and ice..." These gifts allowed Eva to dodge death or injury, live through bombings, invasions and deadly epidemics and avoid completely the horrors that struck other German Jews coming of age during World War II. This book will describe many examples of my mother's resilience and perseverance; traits

1

I believe I have modeled. This book also serves as a coda; the culmination of years of personal work coming to terms with my mother and her sometimes-frustrating ways.

Eva, her brother Gunther, and their parents, my maternal grandparents, left Berlin in 1939, emigrating, like more than 18,000 other German Jews, to Shanghai, China.

According to the definition provided by the U. S. Holocaust Museum, my mother is a survivor of the Holocaust. The official definition is: "A survivor is any persons, Jewish or non-Jewish, who were displaced, persecuted, or discriminated against due to the racial, religious, ethnic, social, political policies of the Nazis and their collaborators from 1933-1945." This definition thus includes Eva and her family. Along with other survivors they lived through and witnessed horrific instances of human depravity. It is a miracle that most of the survivors of the Holocaust lived to be liberated and to begin a new life; many unfortunate souls, who were survivors under this definition, did not live. They simply died of grief or physical or mental illness, or committed suicide.

My mother argues vehemently with me, saying that, in her view, "survivors" are those who were actually deported to the Nazi death camps and survived. I, in turn, reply that no, she too, is considered a survivor. She will then comment that there is no comparison between being in a concentration camp and living in Shanghai as a refugee. I respond that her experience is not being likened to being a prisoner in a camp; that both situations were bad. There is no winning this argument, and I always feel depleted, frustrated, and upset that my opinion and my disagreement with her has caused this angry outburst. I feel guilty having caused my mother to feel sadness and anger. On the other hand, I can understand her resistance to being identified as a Holocaust survivor. She was incredibly fortunate to escape Germany and get to Shanghai, living nine years there.

On a recent trip to Berlin, the following exchange took place between us when I saw a Holocaust memorial listing the names of the death camps and ghettos that included Shanghai. Suddenly, she became very angry at seeing Shanghai on the same wall as Treblinka and the other camps. She said:

"I hate having Shanghai next to the names of the camps.
"I just hate it!
"How can you compare? Warsaw! How can you compare?
"We are alive!"

When we visited the apartment building where she lived as a child in Berlin, I asked her if she wanted a Stolperstein—a commemorative stone with the names of individuals who had lived at a given address before being deported to a camp or other location—placed on the ground outside of the structure. This is now common practice in Germany. She replied:

"No. Oh no no. I don't want that.
"I don't want one of those stones.
"I don't like it."

I believe these statements to be real expressions of her feelings. It is absolutely true that my mother and her mother lived through World War II and many others perished. However, based on my research, I believe her reactions are indicative of "Survivor's Guilt", a syndrome affecting people who lived through a traumatic event where others perished.

I have felt a sadness and discomfort surrounding my mother ever since I can remember. As a child I saw again and again my mother's young, pretty face completely composed but with a fixed expression. There seemed to be something brewing inside of her. While I was a sensitive child, there was no way to ascertain what was going on in her head.

I noticed this aura of loss and vulnerability with other older people who were my grandmothers' friends. To me, it just seemed normal. These older, often distinguished and cultured, men and women, originally from Germany and Austria, had kind but sad faces, sighed a great deal, and shook their heads unconsciously. Even as a young girl, I could tell something was amiss, and I treaded lightly around them. Perhaps, that is why I have never wanted to cause problems for people, an often-maladaptive behavior that has taken me decades to conquer. I was always afraid that these individuals would cry or fall apart. As previously mentioned, this included my mother and maternal grandmother.

My mother's story has always been in the background of my life and in the roles I have taken on, and this then is my mother's story but also my own. I learned directly from my mother what it was to be a woman and a wife. What happened to my mother in her youth placed a shadow on her approach to parenting and that shadow affected me as a young child. This would be an indirect means for which her experiences were transmitted to me. I carry my mother's story with me, for better or worse, and while I am my mother's daughter, I am not she. However, I carry her genes and was raised by her; and like all of us, I received from my mother a version of her burdens, her joys and adventures, and her traumas.

I am proud of my mother, her fortitude and positive outlook. She is quiet and unassuming. She firmly believes that no one will be interested in her story. I think Jews and non-Jews will find this a unique story of resourcefulness in the face of loss, sorrow and great evil. This book is also the story of a daughter; a young girl who grew up in a different time and place and had to find her own path and eventually understand and accept her mother's different ways. I hope this story will capture life as Eva lived it, from

1927 to 1949. I have included chapters on the corresponding years of my life, contrasting my coming of age with hers and elucidating the influences of her experiences on my own thoughts and behavior.

Eva and Karen, 2015.

Chapter 1

KAREN

My mother met my father, Max Levi, in 1949, in San Francisco, less than two years after she arrived in the United States. My father had been born in Konstanz, Germany in 1921 and, having arrived in San Francisco in 1938, was already established there. He had a car and a good job as a salesman.

To hear my mother tell it, my father was quite proud of marrying a so-called sophisticated young woman from Berlin. Even then, in 1949 after everything that had transpired, Berlin had a certain cache among German Jews. On her side, my mother was taken by the dark haired, blue-eyed young man who she says resembled the actor John Garfield.

Eva and Max were married in 1950. They first lived in a small apartment on Haight and Fillmore Streets. My father worked for Mr. Hirschfelder, a German-Jewish man, not a recent immigrant, with a successful wholesale business, selling baker's and confectioner's supplies. My father worked diligently and tirelessly for the company. My mother worked in Franklin Hospital as a Laboratory Technologist. My mother has said that their early married life was happy and that they enjoyed the inexpensive but elaborate meals in the various ethnic neighborhoods of San Francisco and sometimes went dancing and to nightclubs. My father played soccer for a Jewish league, Hakoah, and they seemed to have many young friends that they knew from the Jewish community and from their jobs. When I was growing up approximately 90% of my parents' friends were refugees from Nazi Germany, either coming directly to the United States or via Shanghai, England, or Israel. A few friends were American-born Jews. They had few American-born Christian friends. Limited mixing and mingling is described in the research as a common occurrence among Holocaust survivor families. In my mind, the Shanghai Jews seemed more mysterious, less American; however, I do believe this was a result of the exotic nature of their journey to China, the mystery associated with their history, and their recent arrival when compared to American-born Jews.

Eva and Max Levi, married May 28, 1950, San Francisco.

I was born in 1951, the year after my parents married. The pregnancy was a great surprise, and she almost miscarried at one point. She said that she "really wanted me after that experience". I imagine that the shock of nearly losing me may have triggered severe anxiety on her part, given her history of loss, so my healthy birth must have been a great relief to the entire family. My mother describes me as a "good baby" and a very talkative toddler. I walked very late, and my mother was terribly frightened by a pediatrician who suggested there was something developmentally amiss. However, it turned out I was just a very late walker. My sister, Connie, was born in 1954 and my brother Larry in 1963.

Eva and Karen, 1952.

We were a very small family, with just two living grandmothers; they were Omi (the traditional German diminutive for Grandmother) Kaethe, my mother's mother and Omi Trude, my father's mother, but no aunts, uncles or first cousins. I have few memories of my early childhood, but I know there were family outings and vacations and holidays spent with the grandmothers. One early memory from this period though is hearing Omi Kaethe singing in her lovely clear soprano voice. And my Omi Trude coming to visit me when I was sick and feeling much better after I saw her kind smile.

After their first apartment, my parents bought a building consisting of two flats in San Francisco's Sunset district, a neighborhood of upwardly mobile young families, primarily of Irish and Italian-American descent. We lived in one of the flats. The Sunset is a large section of San Francisco that extends eastward from the Pacific Ocean to the geographic middle of the city, skirting Golden Gate Park. The area consists of single-family houses, duplexes, flats, and apartment buildings. My mother was a housewife who worked part-time at the hospital. I was told we spent our days shopping for groceries, playing in the park, and visiting with other young mothers and their children. I have only vague memories of those days.

Chapter 2

EVA

My mother was born in Berlin, Germany in 1927. Times were relatively good in Germany for my mother's family. My grandfather, Karl, was a businessman, a sales representative and broker. He worked hard and provided well for his family. My grandmother, Kaethe, was a housewife, though as a young girl she had been a star runner in high school and later worked as a nurse for wounded German soldiers in World War I. She loved opera and singing. My mother also had a brother, Gunther, who was five years older than her, a sickly and asthmatic child. My mother describes him as kind, gentle, and well liked. Before my grandparents married, they had already suffered tragedies. My grandmother's two promising brothers, Fritz and Ernst, one a stockbroker and the other an aspiring doctor, were killed in France, within 6 weeks of each other, in World War I. Both grandfathers, Karl and Alfons (paternal) also served in the war.

A cousin on my maternal grandmother's side, Ralph Salinger, has conducted extensive genealogical research tracing this side of my family to a town in East Prussia, known then as Wormditt. The present name of the town is Orneta, and it is in Poland. He was able to trace the family back to my maternal great-great-grandparents, Tobias and Cacile Sandmann, born in 1828 and 1834 respectively. They were born and lived in Wormditt.

My Grandmother Kaethe and my Grandfather Karl, a picture celebrating their upcoming marriage

A postcard from 1899, written by my maternal grandmother's uncle, Emil Sandmann.

The children of Tobias and Cacile Sandmann.
Young girl at top left is Rosa, my great-grandmother.

The family of my maternal grandmother, Kaethe Warschauer Wolffheim, included Cila and Hiam Berkowitz and Paul and Eva Gutfeld who moved from East Prussia to Palestine in the 1920's as pioneers in the Zionist movement. My mother has described this branch of the family as the brave Zionists who wisely left Germany and helped to build the new state of Israel. Other relatives went to England, Sweden, and Peru.

My grandfather Karl was born in Berlin, the son of Salomon and Klara Wolffheim of Berlin. His mother was widowed quite young and raised her four children—Alfred, Emmy, Eugen, and Karl—on her own. According to my mother, her Grandmother Klara was a stern, no-nonsense woman who was tall, slender and not too much fun for a child. Her name is registered as the owner of a boutique for women's fashions, but my mother reported that Emmy "ran the store". Perhaps, Klara started the store and Emmy took over when she was old enough.

Eva's older brother Gunther, born 1922.

My mother's family lived in the Tiergarten neighborhood in West Berlin. From 1929, when she was two years old, until the family fled Germany, she lived at 9 Flotowstrasse. This is a small tree-lined street with the Tiergarten S Bahn station at one end, and the calm river Spree at the other end. In the 1930's, there was a small bakery, with fresh, hot rolls available every morning, across the street. I imagine her family enjoying the crisp small rolls, some round, and some crescent shaped, topped with salt or caraway or poppy seeds. This little district included both the Hansa shopping area and the U Bahn station. My grandmother did her daily shopping in small stores, some of which are still there. The building where my mother and her family lived consists of six large flats, and was not damaged in the Allied bombing, though other sections of Flotowstrasse were. Since reunification many improvements have been made on the street.

9 Flowtostrasse, Berlin, Germany.

My mother and I visited Berlin in 2014. My mother noticed that there are now more cars and trees on her street then she remembered from 75 years earlier. The sidewalks and street are still constructed of stones. 9 Flotowstrasse was built circa 1910-1919 and now has a beautiful art deco design over the entranceway. As I stood in front of the building, I noticed several small brass plaques, inscribed with the names of past residents with a start and end date. I have mentioned earlier; they are the famous Stolperstein or stumbling stones of Germany. The stones are usually inscribed "Hier wohnt", "Here lived." They have been placed in front of buildings where victims of the Holocaust once lived. There were five such plaques on the ground in front of my mother's childhood home.

There is a small central staircase, leading up to the large, wooden front door. One rings a bell for the flat one desires to visit. A small window below ground opened onto the apartment of the porter. As was the custom of the day, he would stick his head out the window when people came to the door to monitor the comings and goings of visitors and residents. His flat was on the parterre level, or what we would call the basement.

With no trouble, just the blink of the eye, I could see the slender quick girl of the 1930's running up the stairs, two at a time. The family flat had a long hall with numerous rooms on both sides, a small living room, bathroom, bedrooms and a servant's room. The hall ended at the 'Berlin Room', a combination dining room and family room. After that there was the kitchen, closed off by a door. The kitchen was medium-sized by our standards. Domestic life was organized differently; everyone had his or her place. The cook and maid were in the kitchen area, and the resident family members were in the other living spaces. The maid or cook rang a bell for dinner; it would have been unthinkable to poke one's head in the kitchen to see if the food was ready. The other distinctive space was the Herrenzimmer—men's room—for the man of the house, a kind of study or office. Off this room was a balcony where meals were taken in summer months. On hot summer days and evenings, my mother has told me how she would run with an empty bowl to buy ice cream at a nearby shop, to be eaten immediately on return.

Beginning in 1933 and lasting until they fled Berlin, more and more space was given over to rental rooms. At first the children had their own bedrooms. When my grandfather lost his business and then all means of making a living, due to Nazi-imposed restrictions, more and more rooms were rented for extra income. Early in this period, my grandparents lost their live-in servants. The cook—"Anna"— was allowed to stay, since she was married and lived with her husband at her own place. Under Nazi regulations, single Christian women were not allowed to live with Jewish families; the theory being that they were in danger from lascivious Jewish men. This cook and her husband were to serve an important role for Grandfather Karl after Kristallnacht.

Chapter 3

KAREN

In 1958, my parents bought a house in the Monterey Heights district of San Francisco. Monterey Heights is a rather affluent section, nestled in the hills, beneath Mt. Davidson, which is a small mountain dominated by a large grey cross. It was somewhat weird to be living almost literally under a cross, being a child who was very aware of being Jewish. It's a well-known San Francisco landmark. Single-family houses characterize the neighborhood, with a variety of styles, sitting on small to moderate-sized lots. Nearby is one of the most affluent areas in the city, St. Francis Wood. The mansions and beautiful large houses on wooded plots of land awed my mother, sister and me. I attended Commodore Sloat Elementary, Aptos Junior High, and Lowell High Schools. The first two were neighborhood public schools. Lowell was an academic high school, and a student needed the Junior High School principal's recommendation to attend. My mother advocated for me with the school principal to attend, since I was not a stellar middle school student. This was one of the best decisions my mother made. I was motivated in the stimulating environment of my high school and became a good student, headed for college.

As a young child and into my preteens, I spent a great deal of time with both of my grandmothers. They helped care for my sister and me, and I have wonderful memories of Saturdays with them. My mother worked on Saturdays in a small laboratory, when the full time staff was off, to make her own money. My father worked on Saturday also. They didn't observe the Sabbath. My sister and I loved to be with our grandmothers; however, we didn't like to be different from our peers who spent their weekends with their parents.

My paternal grandmother—Omi Trude—took us to "the beach" which was Ocean Beach. There was a Playland and hamburger/hot dog joints to enjoy. There was a beautiful little park overlooking the ocean where we could safely run and, once there, get to a walkway and go down a steep hill. My grandmother and sister and I passed a demolished structure, the former Sutro Baths, and the famous Cliff House, as we walked down the hill. Then we strolled by the ocean, along the breakfront. We never actually went on the beach, as it was a cold and windy place. The large waves were forbidding and the sand was brown and dirty. Our grandmothers were rather formal and always were dressed up. They would never have taken off their shoes and walked on the sand. I loved the salt air and clear blue skies and bracing wind. I do not recall a visit when it was a typical grey and damp day. Omi Trude also took us to museums in Golden Gate Park and to the Japanese Tea Garden, another favorite place. I loved to run around the manicured gardens and over the stone bridges, which crossed brooks, bordered by flowers and ornamental greenery. The great treat was sitting down to jasmine tea and cookies, served by pretty Japanese women in colorful kimonos and zoris. I played my own game of picking the prettiest waitress and the prettiest kimono. When we were in Golden Gate Park with my grandmother, Connie and I played dog and master and also loved to dance around on the Bandstand stage.

My maternal grandmother—Omi Kaethe—took us on excursions to Fisherman's Wharf and what was then known as the Aquatic Park, before Ghirardelli Square was developed. My sister and I used to pretend that we were fishing on those trips to the bay front. The wharves and docks were made of slats of weathered wood. We used to taunt ourselves about falling between the wooden slats into the cold bay. Alcatraz loomed in the Bay as a creepy, old, decrepit place. The Aquatic Park area was developed in my teen years and became a destination for teen shopping adventures. In the 1970's, the wharf areas were also developed. San Francisco was a great city for exploring interesting districts and was filled with ethnic neighborhoods, rich in culture and different foods. I was lucky to grow up in such a stimulating environment, and I was exposed to people from different lands, speaking foreign languages.

Karen and Connie, in a quieter moment, 1959, approximately.

Not coincidental I am sure, the ethnic area I was most familiar with was Chinatown. We had Chinese food there, on Friday nights, when I was taking swimming lessons at the Chinese YMCA. I also went to Chinatown on several Girl Scout excursions, with my father to deliver packages of nuts to his Chinese restaurant customers, and for family dinners on special occasions. San Francisco's Chinatown is the best one I have seen, and it is the largest outside of China. Grant Avenue is the main street, decorated with colorful lanterns and neon signs that are lighted up at night. There are restaurants, bakeries, gift shops, vegetable stands, and fish and poultry stores. There was nothing better than looking at the inexpensive treasures in the gift shops—pencil boxes, pencils with tassels and little Chinese people on them, secret boxes, fans, jewelry, screens, lanterns, and furniture.

Omi Kaethe was most probably seriously affected by her experiences in China, and I sensed this as a young child. She suffered from psychological and physical illnesses in San Francisco, likely due to the trauma and deprivation of immigration and life in Shanghai. She was hospitalized in San Francisco several times for Depression. Nevertheless, I have many fond memories of her. I can still see her coming down the hill from the bus to our house, laden with treats for the family. She was always available to help my mother. She had a sense of humor. She was tireless and went to many stores to find the best winter coat for us or whatever it was she was looking for. She was well liked and had many friends. Even though she had her own medical problems, Omi Kaethe was always available to help a less fortunate friend or acquaintance. She always gave us spending money, especially needed as I got older. I always will remember the three one-dollar bills she left on my desk. That was enough money for many purposes. Recently, my sister told me that my mother told her that Omi Kaethe defended me when my father had ostensibly made a critical comment about me. Evidently, this was a source of arguments between them. Until she shared this story, I had no idea that it had occurred.

My other grandmother, Omi Trude, immigrated to San Francisco in 1938. My father's family had relations in California who had "vouched" for them and signed affidavits insuring their support of my father and grandparents. This was the only way for German Jews to gain access to the United States at the time. It was a somewhat easier process but not without its stress. As a result, Omi Trude seemed less traumatized by the time I was born and more acculturated to the United States. She had also been sheltered from World War I having been sent by her parents to England to study. And she had also attended a boarding school in Switzerland prior to the war. It seems that she may have had a more pampered childhood, though not without loss and sadness. After arriving in the United States, this refined lady had to go to work as a Practical Nurse—a nurse's aide—and my paternal grandfather, a former merchant and store owner, was relegated to silver polishing, due to his age and poor English skills. Omi Trude retold her stories to me without complaining and she seemed very appreciative that she could save her family. She had to leave her mother in Germany and this great grandmother was deported to Treblinka and was murdered there. In her last few years, Omi Trude became depressed, agitated and began to lose touch with reality. This could have been a sign of a dementia and/or a reaction to past trauma. According to reports from several family members, she began to be very fearful and angry and spoke a lot about her mother.

Chapter 4

EVA

My mother describes a pleasant life from the time of her birth until 1938. My grandfather was a successful salesman and broker for large companies that sold cotton knit clothes, such as t-shirts and pajamas, and he had an office in Alexanderplatz. Berlin was a cultured, sophisticated city, with a well-known demimonde as well. The city was known for its museums, concerts, and fine restaurants. My mother remembers her parents going to concerts, restaurants, nightclubs, movies, on nice vacations and, specifically, to the nearby Biergarten.

Though outside the experience of my mother's family, there were also places in the city where certain "degenerate", as the Nazis called them, subcultures flourished—modern art, jazz, homosexuality, leftist politics, and anti-establishment literature. New freedoms in Weimar Germany after World War I triggered an explosion of "sexual exuberance" of every type, according to the writer Edgar Ansel Mower. He noted: "It is hard to conceive a much more tolerant society." The popular play and movie, "Cabaret", based on Christopher Isherwood's stories, also depicts this period vividly.

While it may be difficult to believe that Nazism flourished in this environment, despite the traditional cultural and artistic atmosphere, most Germans were suffering terribly due to the worldwide depression, economic restraints imposed on Germany after World War I and massive unemployment. Hitler entered this milieu just at the precisely perfect time and had a meteoric rise to power, also in part due to a very weak government in place. Most Germans did not believe Hitler would reach a powerful position and when he did, it was thought that he would not last long. Latent anti-Semitism was always present in Germany, so it didn't take much to convince the German people that their troubles were caused by, what they saw, as affluent, well-off Jews. The Jews still believed that their military service in World War I and their loyalty to Germany during peaceful times would temper the extreme anti-Semitic rhetoric. However, this was not to be. Violence escalated a few months after Hitler came to power. The early problems, such as the anti-Jewish boycott on April 1, 1933, were a harbinger of ominous events to come.

The nearby Biergarten my grandparents frequented is still standing with both an outside and inside section. The inside section is a Bier Quelle or cave, which we would know as a pub, dark and subdued. The outside part consists of small tables set among a grove of trees that are illuminated by strands of round light bulbs. There is a small hut where the beer and simple food are prepared, such as pretzels, salads, and sausages.

In contrast to the simplicity of the local Biergarten, my grandmother entertained at home in high style. My mother remembers shopping trips to the food emporium at KDW (Kaufhaus des Westens), a famous German department store, still open for business. There my grandmother bought delicacies and gourmet delights for fancy dinner parties.

My mother was allowed to roam freely in her neighborhood when she was as young as 8, attending birthday parties and visiting with friends. She attended coeducational public schools until Nazi regulations prohibited this in 1936 and then went to a variety of Jewish schools. My mother even attended summer camps in nearby Czechoslovakia. Because of his frail health, her brother, Gunther, attended boarding schools in Switzerland and Austria.

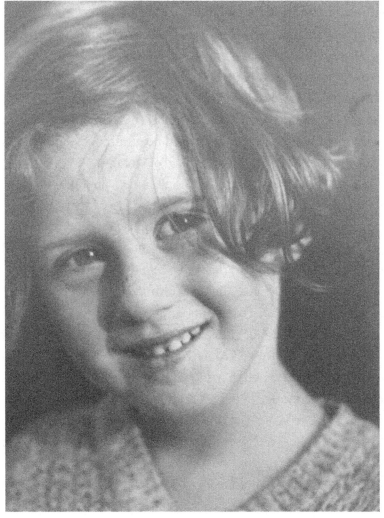

Eva, age 5 or 6.

My grandfather's brothers and sister were in and out of the Wolffheim Berlin apartment, and my mother has vivid memories of them. Most notable was Uncle Eugen. He had married a Christian woman, Elspeth, but she seems to have converted to Judaism at some point. Eugen was a colorful businessman and adventurer, with many female admirers. This latter observation comes directly from my mother's ears and eyes, in other words what she witnessed as a child. My mother's childish recollection seems to be corroborated by actual evidence. Based on reports from a descendent of Elspeth, government documents, and newspaper advertisements, the couple traveled to the United States in 1909. They were married in Germany immediately before they left for the United States. Eugen and Elspeth were an unusual couple for their time. Eugen and Elspeth raised beautiful dogs in Germany, according to my mother, who recalled them as "Wolfhounds". When they arrived in the United States, Eugen and Elspeth began to train dogs again.

While in the United States, Elspeth had her own Vaudeville act called, "Elsie La Bergere and Posing Dogs". I was told that Elspeth was approached on the street and asked if she would like to be in a Vaudeville act. This may or may not be true, but there are pictures and advertisements in newspapers that show that the couple had a Vaudeville act. Eugen was Elspeth's manager. They became naturalized American citizens in 1922 in Queens, New York, but returned that same year to their life in Berlin. According to my mother, Eugen's mother, Klara, had wanted them to return to Berlin.

They bought a large house in the affluent suburb of Schoneiche, near Berlin, and Eugen became the director of a wholesale dental supply firm, Delakur. When the Nazis came to power, Eugen attempted to transfer the company over to a Christian friend, but the government wouldn't allow this transaction. The Nazis took over the company in 1938.

Had they stayed in the United States, they might have been able to bring the remainder of the family on an affidavit of agreed support. My mother once said, "If he had brought us to New York, we wouldn't have had to 'go through Shanghai'". She didn't continue her thought, but I silently wondered, as people do on hearing a mother or father use the word "if", would her brother Gunther have lived and would I have been born?

U.S. Passport application for Eugen and Elspeth Wolffheim.

A few months before the "November—Aktion, 1938 (how the Germans referred to Kristallnacht), Elspeth had visited a rabbi in Berlin to proclaim herself as a Jew and take classes. She also presented herself as a Christian to attempt to help her husband in some way. In any event, Eugen and Elspeth's house was damaged and ransacked on Kristallnacht.

Another notable relative in my mother's memory was her father's sister, Aunt Emmy. Emmy was divorced from her husband

and was a successful, stylish businesswoman, both rare situations even in avant-garde 1930s Berlin. At first she was a buyer for a department store and then she was the owner-manager of her mother's boutique. According to my mother, Emmy was always trying to dress her sister-in-law, my grandmother, in stylish clothes, as evidently, my grandmother did not care much about fashion. Emmy's son, Hans, was sent to Shanghai and eventually married Elfie, another Shanghai Jew. They came to live in San Francisco. They had a son, Robert, who I played with as a child. Unfortunately, Emmy Wolffheim remained in Germany, ultimately dying in a concentration camp.

Source:	Gedenkbuch - Opfer der Verfolgung der Juden unter der nationalsozialistischen Gewaltherrschaft in Deutschland 1933-1945, Bundesarchiv (German National Archives), Koblenz 1986
Last Name:	Wolffheim
First Name:	Emma
Date of Birth:	17/11/1883
Permanent Place of Residence:	Berlin,Berlin,Berlin,Germany 🔍 📍
Place of Death:	Auschwitz,Camp,Poland 🔍 📍
Status in the source:	missing
Type of material:	List of murdered Jews from Germany
Item ID:	3871775

Indicates an automatic translation from Hebrew

Record of Emmy's death in Auschwitz
(document copied from German National Archives).

According to my mother's memory, the oldest of my grandfather's siblings, Alfred, was banished by the family for some reason. He went to sea in the merchant marines and rose to be a Captain for the African German Line, a very respectable position in those days. So it appears that the Wolffheim branch of the family was quite independent and adventurous with the exception of my Grandfather Karl. My mother once said, "We (speaking of her immediate family) were the only 'normal' ones."

My grandmother's role slowly evolved in the 1930's. At the beginning of her married life, she was the wife of a successful businessman. As time went on, she received more training as a nurse, in preparation for what she must have seen as uncertain times ahead.

She had two children, raised in a strict hands-off approach, common in those days. Children were expected to behave and not participate in adult activities. It was an adult-oriented life, not a child-centered existence such as one finds in modern American life. The children, however, were exposed to excellent, enriching experiences. My mother provided me with several anecdotes that seem incredible to me but are indicative of how different the times were. Little Eva was put on a train, with a group of children and chaperones, and sent to a summer camp in Denmark at the age of five and in the former Czechoslovakia at the age of six or seven! My mother was allowed to travel on the subway when she was nine years old. Eva walked alone through a park and over a river as a young child. Most surprising of all was the story of my grandparents going out at night to have a beer in a Bier Quelle— a pub still in the same spot—and leaving my primary school aged mother home alone. My mother said she stood watch over the street by standing at a window and looking out until she saw my grandparents returning home. Then my mother dashed to her room and was asleep before her parents checked in on her.

Omi Kaethe went to coffee with friends, shopped, and super-vised social events at home, sometimes taking my mother to visit "the aunts"; these were the sisters of my grandmother's mother. My great grandmother, Rosa, was a short, plump, cheery grand-mother to my mother. Rosa had six sisters and two brothers. Some of these siblings died before my mother was old enough to meet them or remember them. They produced many offspring, who spread all over the world, just barely ahead of the Nazis. Aunt Ida married Louis Salinger. Their son was Ernst. He moved to England and married. The child from this marriage is Ralph, who is my mother's second cousin. Ralph was raised in New Zealand and now lives in Israel. Aunt Hedwig's family went to Sweden. And, as previously mentioned, Aunt Blanca's and Aunt Agathe's children immigrated to Palestine.

Kaethe was in charge of the care of the children and was particularly involved in the upbringing of Gunther. He required special medical treatment and attended boarding schools in high altitude, dry environments, places considered essential for asthmatics in the days prior to the inhalers and medicines of today. While the state of care for asthma in the 1920's and 1930's was fairly advanced and treatments included a variety of experimental drugs, including adrenalin, asthmatics were advised to live in smoke-free environments with good air circulation and reduced air pollution, hence the mountains. Humidity was not considered advisable, as mold and other irritants were rampant in moist places. My grandmother even took Gunther to a psychologist as asthma attacks were often brought on by stress.

Gunther Wolffheim,
age 9 approximately.

Eva told me that her brother, Gunther, was a sweet person who had loyal, intelligent friends. Eva, being the little sister, admired and 'flirted' with his friends, to the extent a girl of 10 flirts. She was smitten with one young man, Erick, who took her on a 'date' to KDW for an ice cream. She recounts that she was so flabbergasted she didn't say a word during the entire outing.

My Grandmother Kaethe took my mother to Jewish High Holiday services at different large, Reform synagogues in Berlin. These synagogues, on Fasenstrasse, Oranienbergerstrasse, and Levetzowstrasse, established the models for Reform synagogues into the late 20th century. My mother describes a large congregation, rabbis and cantors, and sometimes a choir. My mother said that there was a famous Rabbi Wolf who the women admired due to his good looks and urbane qualities. The services were in German. The congregation was the audience and the rabbis and cantor were the leaders. Sermons were informative and intellectually stimulating. The cantors were classically trained singers who sang in an operatic style. My mother also reported that she and her friend Ruth would walk to the synagogue on Levetzowstrasse for children's services.

As the dangers increased in Berlin, it became obvious to my grandparents that great changes were in store for them. They prepared to take up careers and jobs in a new, as-yet-unknown, place. As stated previously, my grandmother attended nursing classes at the Nursing Hospital of the Jewish Congregation in Berlin. She had been a nurse during World War I, but she knew that she needed to learn new skills. My grandfather found different products to sell in different ways.

The prohibitions for the Jews were formalized in the Nuremberg Laws in 1935 and increased significantly with the events of 1938. It has been noted many times that the changes imposed by the Nazis were gradual and the German Jews were in what the modern world would call a state of denial. Denial has been noted as a common response to rapid change, and it may have been easy for Jews to ignore what was happening even though, in hindsight, it seems obvious. Even while my grandfather's successful career gradually diminished, he always was able to bring money into the household.

Kaethe Wolffheim, as a nurse in World War I.

It is a common, and cruel, fallacy that German Jews sat back, enjoyed their nice lives, and then complacently walked into the Nazi train cars headed for extermination camps. Starting in 1935, with the establishment of the Nuremberg Laws, German Jews immediately formed or strengthened Jewish Community Centers and synagogues to provide a wide variety of social and recreational services for the German Jews and large numbers of Jews streaming into Germany from areas to the East, such as Poland and Russia. There were schools, athletic clubs, recreational activities, vocational skills training, concerts, lectures, etc. The more established Jews in Berlin set up housing and food services for the poorer immigrants coming in from countries to the east. My mother said that she remembered seeing these people, from the shtetls and small villages of Russia and Poland, dressed differently than the big city dwellers.

These, "Eastern" Jews spoke different languages, including Yiddish, and practiced Judaism and celebrated holidays differently. They lived primarily in what had been the former Jewish neighborhoods of Berlin, as the more affluent German Jews had been moving outward to other areas. As we know, this is a common occurrence in urban and suburban areas all over the developed world, and there is always a potential for judgment or conflict between the sophisticated, well-established citizens and the newly-arrived rural immigrants. This is a cultural phenomenon that will probably never change.

When my mother began school in 1932, in honor of the event, she was given a Schultute, the traditional large paper cone, filled with goodies that would delight any 5-6 year old in the world. This was and continues to be a German tradition. So vivid were my mother's descriptions of the Schultute, that when I was recently in Berlin, I wanted to buy one for myself! I happened to come across the cones in various stores. A photo—I once saw but cannot locate now—from her first day of school shows Eva in the short, probably scratchy, wool coat of the time and a pretty dress, with a stylish 1930's haircut. She was able to attend the public school until approximately 1936, when the Nuremberg Laws forbid Jewish children from attending regular schools. My mother particularly remembered one public school teacher who "loved Hitler" and made the students salute "Sieg Heil" and sing various Nazi songs at every possible occasion. My mother grimaces every time she tells the story.

After 1936, my mother attended a variety of Jewish schools. This was the first of many steps, which banned Jews from the mainstream of society. Around this time, she was also forbidden to play with her best friend who was Christian. My mother reported that she does not remember who told her not to play with this little girl anymore, either the girl's parents or Eva's parents. This was part of the general campaign by the Nazis to dehumanize the Jews, including the children. In addition to transferring to Jewish schools and being prohibited from going to playgrounds, Jewish children were ostracized by children and parents who had been brainwashed by Nazi propaganda. Sometimes, German children were cruel, for example cleaning the seats where Jewish children sat. Other times, it was understood by parents that one's child was not welcome in a Christian household anymore. My mother said that this was very upsetting to her, but as she was, and still is, very social, she made other "best friends". My mother describes herself as a mediocre elementary school student who was frequently punished for mischievous behavior, even slapped on the hand with a ruler for acting up.

Of course, my mother was much more comfortable in the Jewish school and enjoyed all of the extra-curricular activities. The early experiences my mother had in these Jewish schools and recreational centers most probably set a strong inner foundation that she could return to countless times in her long life. Even though she is not a strictly observant Jew, she has always strongly identified with Jews and the culture and religion. Certainly in Shanghai and then again in the United States, it was the Jewish community that came to the aid of my mother and grandmother.

She describes this time as her first recognition of being singled out and separated. She seemed to be happy but still aware of the undercurrent of discrimination and hatred. Eva continued to run and skip her way through life, visiting her friends, going on outings, and walking through the Tiergarten—a large park and home to the zoo—to school. Berlin hosted the Summer Olympics in 1936, and my mother still remembers the pride she felt when

Jesse Owens ran, won his medal, and beat the German (Nazi supported) runners. To this day, Eva is enamored of the Olympics and watches each and every one on television.

My mother personally experienced both the spontaneous and organized events of the Nazi regime, either by being there, through newsreel, on the radio, or in the newspapers. As a little girl, she was forced to salute and say, "Sieg Heil", sing "Deutschland Uber Alles", and listen to Hitler's hysterical speeches and the screaming, adoring, crowds. She is still very reluctant to go anywhere there is a crowd and becomes visibly distressed when she confronts large groups of people. Understandably, she mistrusts large crowds and "what can happen when things get out of control".

The Wolffheim family went on vacations as long as they were able and went to spots in Germany and Switzerland. The parents went a bit further on their own, to Italy, for example. On the last vacation to the Schwartz Wald—The Black Forest—the family was settled into a fashionable hotel. Soon after they arrived, they had to leave; the manager of the hotel told them "I am very sorry, but Jews are not allowed here". During this time, my grandfather took my mother out on occasion to the Hotel Kempinski in Berlin, a safe excursion as it was owned by Jews. They would have dinner and Grandfather Karl taught little "Evchen" (nickname for Eva) how to comport herself in the finer places. My mother told me that he also taught her about eating cheese—"just a bit"—after a big meal, "even if you are full", telling her the old German saying, "Kaese schliesst den Magen" (Cheese shuts the stomach.).

The family took long walks in the park and Karl would retell the plots of all of the movies he saw with his wife, my grandmother. Movies were the most modern form of entertainment at the time. My mother describes running down an adjacent street near her house to read the notices on the kiosk that advertised the movies that were playing.

This period of 1936-1938 was also the time the family developed the "Umbrella" signal. At this time, when Jews could go to some places but not others, my mother would run ahead with an umbrella. She was fair-haired and looked the "least Jewish" of all of the family members. If my mother opened the umbrella, Jews were permitted in the restaurant or inn. In other words, there was no sign prohibiting Jews. If my mother closed the umbrella or kept it in the closed position, there was a sign and it was "verboten"—forbidden—for Jews to patronize the establishment. Using a child to signal with an umbrella shows the fear, embarrassment and sense of shame that my grandparents must have felt. These feelings are natural in such an environment; especially since showing anger would have resulted in serious consequences.

Chapter 5

KAREN

No one ever spoke to me about my family's history during my early years, but I can remember the word "Shanghai" being uttered quietly by my beloved paternal grandmother and other family friends. I would hear them say, "Kaethe and Eva were in Shanghai. And they lost Gunther and Karl" and they would nod their heads sadly and say, "Tsk, tsk, what a shame." The result was that as a child in the late 1950's, and early 1960's, old enough to be more cognizant of abstract emotions and situations, I came to think that "Shanghai" was somehow shameful and my mother (Eva) and Grandmother (Omi) Kaethe were marked—and not in a positive way—by the experience.

Eventually my mother told me that she and her family had been lucky enough to escape from Germany to China. On occasion my parents spoke fondly of their own childhood memories in Germany, gathering wild berries, ice-skating and drinking hot chocolate. I have always had a vivid imagination, so I could see in my mind's eye the bursting berries and taste the creamy, chocolaty hot drink after skating in the cold. My mother had a brooch of a person on broken skis. When I asked her what the pin meant, she told me of the time she broke her brother's skis. I vaguely remember seeing a small leather pouch on a string, to be worn around the neck, in one of my mother's drawers. I believe my mother wore it, with the purpose of carrying some money out of Germany. Other times, when my father talked about his past or I asked a question, my mother would close up, get a tight look on her face, and not say much.

As a child I was highly aware and verbal. I even understood German, so I am sure I picked up quite a bit of information indirectly or subliminally as well as directly when the adults spoke in German. Of course, I don't remember these occasions very well. However, children gain a great deal of information about their parents—their concerns, fears, feelings, opinions—just by listening and being in the same house. Children know who is angry and who is carefree, for example. Martin Goldsmith, the author of *The Inextinguishable Symphony* and the child of Holocaust survivors of German descent, describes an invisible tree growing in his house. This massive tree, with deep roots, grew and "overshadowed" all aspects of his growing-up years. Of course, the tree was not real. It represented the unspoken stories and unexpressed emotions regarding his parents' past.

It is possible that unconscious experiences can also be transmitted from parents to their children through some complex process of extra-sensory communication, according to Dr. Natan Kellerman (who is studying these phenomena). He goes on to say that, "In fact, such quasi-naturalistic terminology is frequently applied when describing how the 'vibrations' within a Holocaust family 'atmosphere' may affect the offspring in a variety of indirect and subtle ways."

Research is currently being done all over the world on the effects of parental communication in Holocaust survivors on their offspring. However, there is rarely a clear and simple linear connection between parent and child. The method of transmission of information between the first and second generation is seen as multifaceted. The mechanism by which trauma is communicated is influenced by the nature of the parent-child relationship as determined by the Holocaust context; the historical imagery provided by the parent and by other cultural processes, such as religious school and secular school; normative developmental conflicts; overall family dynamics independent of the Holocaust; and level of education, social class, nationality, and religious and cultural identity. Overall, research is supporting the anecdotal evidence that Holocaust survivors have functioned adequately as parents, though they have transmitted aspects of their unique experiences to their children in specific ways.

I believe that my mother's grief was conveyed to me. Professionals have named this phenomenon "trans-generational grief". Four major theoretical approaches to understanding trauma transmission have been suggested, based on a review of relevant literature by Dr. Kellerman: 1. Psychodynamic—the medium is interpersonal interaction and the result is an emotion which has been displaced onto a child; 2. Sociocultural—the medium is socialization and the result is a transmission of role models; 3. Family system—the medium is communication and the result is enmeshment; and 4. Biological models of transmission—the medium is genetic and the result is a hereditary susceptibility to Post-Traumatic Stress Disorder (PTSD). One of the mechanisms by which trans-generational grief is transmitted is by the "Conspiracy of Silence". This would fall under the category of "family system". According to Judith Kestenberg, a researcher on the Holocaust, trauma and the concomitant grief is passed down the generations concealed by a cloak of silence. Sometimes there is a total lack of words. Parents may say that they are shielding their children from terrifying horrors—when they are actually protecting themselves, purposely forgetting the past, and/or starting a new life. Sometimes, there is an excess of words, yet there is a silence or an apparent unawareness about the underlying traumas, guilt, shame, and meanings the parents made of their history. Broaching this silence can bring severe responses of anger or hurt, leading in turn to retreat from hurting parents who have already been hurt so much. The latter is a situation I frequently encountered with my mother. For many years, when I tried to ask questions or show my interest in Shanghai, my mother would become agitated. The "conspiracy of silence" may be a major reason for the difficulty many children of Holocaust survivors have when trying to connect their vague sensations of fear, sadness and vulnerability with actual memories of the experience of growing up with Holocaust survivor parents. It took me many years to understand the relationships between my fears and my parents' experiences.

Genetic transmission of trauma has been studied in recent years, for example with Holocaust survivors and their children, Cambodian refugees and their offspring and the children of 9/11 survivors. Rachel Yehuda has been in the forefront of this research. Her studies based on Holocaust offspring revealed that the children of PTSD-stricken mothers were diagnosed with PTSD three times as often as members of control groups. Children of fathers or mothers with PTSD suffered three to four times as much depression and anxiety, and engaged more in substance abuse. Dr. Yehuda would go on to discover that children of mothers of survivors of the Holocaust and 9/11 had less cortisol than a control group. Cortisol is a steroid hormone, which is vital in regulating stress on a physiological level.

Social science researchers have studied the lack of emotionality in survivors of the Holocaust and the stress this has caused for their children. Often, the children complained of somatic (recurrent and multiple medical symptoms with no discernible organic cause) disturbances to obtain attention from their parents. As a child I had many unexplained physical ailments over the years; complaints that did not elicit any sympathy from my mother. Left to my own devices, my coping mechanisms centered on relieving excessive worrying and I turned to reference books to get the answers to my health concerns. I also recall feeling that I only received special attention from my mother when I was truly ill. So as miserable as I felt and as much as I dreaded a penicillin shot, I liked the fact that it meant being sick and staying home from school. And, looking back, it seems my mother could tell the difference between worrying about illness and actually being ill.

I relived this dynamic in 2011 when I was my sister's stem cell donor. My sister, Connie, and I lay on a bed. She was sick with leukemia and I was achy and weak from the shots I received to increase my stem cell production. There was my mother, at age 84, waiting on us.

Once in a while my mother would blurt out a memory, saying things like, "Did you know my friend died at 12, and my other friend, Vera, died of a brain tumor?" For her, there may have been a context for these comments, such as a letter from a relative, a date, or a memory; however, for me there was no such background information. As a child, these remarks would make me feel vulnerable and confused, but I stored them in my memory. Years later, I would think, "And why did she tell me?" I am fairly certain that my mother's sporadic retelling of tragic events led to the development of my own, second-generation, survivor's guilt.

Survivor's Guilt or Survivor's Syndrome, now a recognized symptom of Post-Traumatic Stress Disorder, or PTSD, has been researched widely. Generally speaking, survivor's guilt is a feeling of guilt and anxiety in a survivor of trauma. The individual is relieved to have lived through an accident, disaster, or war; however, he/she asks the question, "Why me? Why did I survive?" In the book, *Mental Health, Social Mirror*, in the chapter "Race and Mental Health", trans-generational survivor's guilt is discussed among various groups. The researchers found that the children of survivors of trauma were as mentally healthy as the control group, though more vulnerable to anxiety, mistrust, and difficulty in expressing anger, as well as somatization.

I still suffer from anxiety and it is still difficult for me to express anger and disagreement with others. My somatization issues are always lying in wait; my body tends to react to stress with physical symptoms, and I tend to worry about my health. In another publication, *Human Adaptation to Extreme Stress: From the Holocaust to Vietnam*, many research studies are summarized. These studies support the hypothesis that the children of survivors of the Holocaust shared common issues growing up. The offspring of the survivors reported an intimacy between parent and child, characterized by a wish for more communication. Not until I became a middle-aged adult did I have the courage to start asking my mother about her life. According to these studies, children of survivors feel protective of their parents and wish to minimize anxiety. I was very conscious of not wanting to cause stress in my parents and was an excessively obedient child, not in any way adventurous until I went to college. I was not particularly rebellious either. Eventually I had to learn—and still today am constantly re-learning—to tolerate any anxiety my actions may cause in others.

In the field of study concerned with survivors and their children, worries about money were reported, as well. An ongoing motif in my own childhood was a struggle over money, with my father never wanting anything new and my mother earning her own money for any extra expenses. When my mother did use "her" money, she was extremely careful, and to this day, she does not buy impulsively or spontaneously. She literally counts every penny. Since having sufficient funds was the key to escape and survival in 1930's Germany, it makes sense that my parents would want to save, looking toward the next catastrophe. Although my father did quite well financially and my mother always supplemented the family finances, the anxiety about finances was constant. Sound practices, such as saving, not allowing expenditures to be higher than incoming funds, not taking out loans, are valuable lessons to be learned for life; however, withholding pleasures, gifts, treats and enriching experiences can lead to very destructive situations in individuals, marriages, and families. When I was a child, the tension about spending reached the point of negativity. There were many arguments and feelings of deprivation among our family members. There was also a great deal of secrecy about who got money from where and what special funds were being used. These are not functional practices for life. They stem from fears about not having enough money, which in our case was not truly realistic.

It is well established that anxiety about money and the fear of spending money, with its various manifestations, can be transmitted from parent to child through socialization or social learning. A child learns various rules, practices, and prohibitions through a parent's child rearing practices. My siblings and I have had ongoing issues regarding money. I have had to struggle with spending all of my life. I do buy items for my house and clothing and jewelry. I go on trips and have experiences as much as I am financially able. I know that life is short and uncertain. However, there is always guilt and anxiety lurking in the background. These distracting emotions never leave me though I have learned to ignore the feelings. My sister and brother seem to have similar experiences, based on my observations and conversations with them.

Another interesting fact I learned reading the academic literature was that the burden of being a survivor's child often fell on the first-born. In my family, as the eldest, it seems that this is the case. Neither of my siblings reflect nor share the same anxieties I have experienced or the intense interest I possess about my mother's story.

Brother, Larry, born in 1963, picture from 1972 approximately.

Larry Levi, 2012.

As I learned more about the difficulties they had faced, and partly due to my incomplete and childish perceptions, my grandparents' and parents' lives were part adventure and part horror. I looked up World War II in the encyclopedia and in books to try to understand, but that, obviously was only part of the story. I poured over the pictures of World War II in the World Book Encyclopedia and I am sure I saw many images in *Look* and *Life* magazines. Given my sensitive nature, I fully expected World War III to start up when I was in the fourth, fifth, and sixth grades. The Cuban Missile Crisis was especially chilling for me. I was eleven years old in October 1962 and, based on my reading on World War II, I was sure we would go to war. I still remember a warm October afternoon, looking up into a clear blue sky, and feeling very unsettled about what was going to happen. This was during the period of bomb shelters and movies shown in school about hiding under our desks in case of bomb attacks. Since I was the child who took all warnings literally, I remember that I couldn't understand why no one else seemed particularly worried, except the newscaster and newspapers. I believe these fears and worries stemmed from a biological susceptibility to anxiety. They were also a result of the stories about World War II that had accumulated in my mind. In addition, I could not fathom a world in which I would be spared or shielded from the miseries my parents experienced.

I was also fascinated with the 1906 San Francisco Earthquake and Fire. I read many children's books about that disaster, which led me to worry that we would have another one. I was extremely nervous each April 18th, the anniversary of the disaster, until well into my high school years. I am still wary of earthquakes and left San Francisco partly because the city and much of California, lies on very active faults. As a child, fire was another one of my fears. In the fifth grade I had seen a frightening movie about fire prevention. From that time on until my early adult years, I was vigilant about a fire starting in my house. I knew from my reading that fire was a big part of World War II—firebombs and crematoriums, and I must have felt that the fires of the war were still burning in me or about to ignite again. These types of fears are cognitive in nature and are characterized by the fear that another catastrophe will occur. There is a preoccupation with death on the part of the survivor's child. The fear serves as a vicarious sharing of Holocaust experiences, which come to dominate the youngster's inner world.

The irony of all this is that my mother does not appear a bit afraid of earthquakes, fire, natural gas leaks, wind, the dark or potentially dangerous people,. These are all fears I had as a child. When I complained, as a child, about the wind at night, she would ignore my fear, and say that she did not hear anything. Not exactly sensitive—and I didn't understand at the time—but what else would one expect from someone who slept through bombings? She would sleep through wind and rainstorms, sending me back to bed when I was scared. She walked through Skid Row without the blink of an eye. And I am not even sure she held my hand when we walked past "winos" in a rough area of downtown San Francisco, which we crossed because we had parked far away to save money. But really, why should she be afraid of a loud storm or a moderate earthquake when she had already seen what humans could do to each other? While she is unfazed by natural disasters and power outages, she does get very upset about man's cruelty to others and to animals.

As a child, I witnessed this fear and caution on the part of my paternal grandmother. Even though Omi Trude had an easier time coming to the United States, she was still traumatized by her experiences. Leaving one's home and losing one's social status in middle age cannot be easy. She always whispered anything related to being Jewish if we were talking in public. I was confused as a child, but now I understand where the apprehension originated. Anyone living in an environment where your religion and ethnic identity could result in humiliation, separation from family and friends, and possible death would be frightened to speak freely in public. Facial expression or simple modeling, to a child, can communicate an adult's fear nonverbally. The continued caution may be quite unnecessary in a different time and place, but it, nonetheless, persists.

Chapter 6

EVA

It is important to point out that my mother's retelling of the Berlin portion of her story is drawn from the memories of a child. No other perspective would be possible as she left Germany at age 11. Her German language skills were also at the level of an 11 year old. She had started to study English before she left Germany, continuing in earnest in Shanghai. Her formal schooling in Shanghai was from a British curriculum and she had British teachers in Shanghai. When she arrived in the United States, she spoke English with a British accent.

Europe has changed dramatically since World War II. She has had to reeducate herself about European cities and ways of life, brush up on her German, and learn, in some cases for the first time, the stories emerging about the Holocaust and World War II. I have to wonder how mind-boggling the changes in Germany and China are for her, after being away for so long. Both places show hardly any resemblance to what they were like in the 1930's. Interestingly, my mother found Berlin, which had been heavily bombed, to be more familiar than Shanghai. Though in Shanghai, she was able to walk directly to her old flat after a cab in Hongkew dropped us off.

Eva was probably aware of growing danger in Berlin, but felt protected by her family, as is typical for children. She apparently took the changes she experienced in stride, making friends easily and being resilient and self-confident by nature. As an example, she will tell anyone that the most traumatic situations in Germany for her were being prohibited from visiting the zoo, or playgrounds, going to ice cream shops and playing with her Christian friends.

It is well known that many German Jews converted to Christianity, either to marry or for social and economic reasons. My grandfather's brother, Alfred, who lived in Hamburg, converted to Christianity when he married a Christian woman. Consequently, this branch of the family is not Jewish. They were spared by the Nazis. Other than that, I do not know of any other family members who converted to Christianity. Alfred was a ship's captain and this thrilled my mother when she was a child. She was enamored of adventure. My mother and grandmother were very fond of Alfred's daughter, Kaethe, and we still have contact with Alfred's granddaughter, Susann.

There are numerous accounts of Jewish families in Germany with Christmas trees in their homes, during the 19th and early 20th centuries. My mother has said that her family "might have had a tree", but adds that it was "for the maid". She has also said, "Everyone celebrated Christmas as a holiday; we just didn't do the religious part". She describes Christmas dinners with special foods such as a roast goose, stolen (heavy fruit cake), lebkuchen (gingerbread), and herring salad for New Year's Eve or Day.

By the autumn of 1938, life in Germany, and especially in Berlin, was extremely difficult. The Anschluss— Nazi invasion of Austria—and occupation of the Sudetenland of Czechoslovakia had occurred and Jews of Germany and Austria were living a shadow existence, discriminated in all sectors of life—social, economic, educational, recreational. My mother was 11 years old and probably reaching the end of primary school. Traditionally, this was the time when students were deciding about the course of their future education. There was a fairly rigid school system in Germany and not everyone was destined to a college track. Many students happily matriculated to a less rigorous curriculum and eventual placement in a trade school of some sort. There was no such transition event for my mother. Under Nazi law, she was prohibited from the German school system. Very soon, other concerns dominated my mother's family as the lives of the Jews were to be put into mortal danger.

November 9-10, 1938 was Kristallnacht—the Night of Broken Glass—when SS mobs and Nazi youth groups destroyed Jewish businesses and homes all over Germany, Austria, and the Sudetenland. Eva's family's house was not attacked and, thankfully, they were not injured. As mentioned, her Uncle Eugen's home was not spared. The Nazis ransacked it, and Eugen, along with 25,000 Jewish men, were taken to Potsdam and then on to a concentration camp, though later released. The Jewish school my mother now attended was burned, so she was at home the following days. One of these days, at lunchtime, plainclothes Gestapo authorities rang the flat at Flotowstrasse 9, and 11-year-old Eva answered the door. The men inquired about her father, my grandfather, asking if he was home and saying they wanted to speak with him. He wasn't home, but the men said that they would return. My mother knew enough to recognize that these men represented a threat, and after they left, my mother ran about two blocks to the Tiergarten S Bahn station. Her father was just on the platform, about to walk home. She told him what had happened and he immediately boarded the subway and went to the Jewish Hospital where his wife, my Grandmother Kaethe, was training. According to my mother, he stayed at the hospital for one night and then went to stay with the family of the Christian maid/cook and was sheltered by them for about two weeks. Thus, my grandfather was saved from certain imprisonment by the Nazis. That was likely the turning point for my grandparents, and from November 1938 until they finally left in April 1939, plans were developed and set in motion to leave Germany. My mother told me that she does not remember most of the details about her father's stay with the maid's family. Nor does she recall their last name or circumstances. This is probably due to the fact that her parents did not speak openly about his hiding place to protect everyone involved.

It was still a time when the Nazis were glad to be rid of the Jews and encouraged their emigration. They saw the Jews' possessions and financial capital as German property and had no intention of permitting refugees to take anything of material value with them. Most Jews who fled had to give up titles to homes and businesses. As previously mentioned, Eugen and Elspeth's home and business were seized, but as my grandparents rented their flat, they didn't lose property. The Jewish emigrants were subject to increasingly heavy taxes that reduced their assets even further. In addition, German officials limited the amount of money that could be transferred abroad from German banks and allowed each passenger to take only ten Reichsmarks (about US $4) out of the country. Many German Jews who managed to emigrate were completely impoverished by the time they were able to leave.

Der Hilfsverein der Juden in Deutschland (Aid Association of German Jews) assisted Jews with their emigration plans. Though they were hampered by the Nazis at every juncture, they still attempted to maintain German thoroughness with a Jewish heart. This organization was established in 1901 to help with needy Jews, primarily coming from eastern European countries. It functioned until 1941 when the Nazis finally prohibited emigration of Jews.

I have asked my mother about the specifics of the family's assets, how much was stolen, sold, etc. She responds that she doesn't know. Of course, adults wouldn't share that information with children and if they had, it would probably be quickly forgotten by a child. Eva had far more interesting ideas swimming in her head. Always an adventurous child and a reader of popular books, such as those by Rudyard Kipling and Robert Louis Stevenson, she was excited by the prospect of traveling to parts unknown, in this case China. She has recounted many times how the children in the Jewish school she attended all shared where they were traveling to flee the Nazis. Each classmate shared his/her destination, such as Britain, Belgium, France, and the Netherlands. When my mother stood up and proudly said, "China", the students and teacher were aghast. "China, how awful, what is there?" they reportedly questioned. Of course, my mother could not really respond and none of them had any way of knowing that China was to prove a safer place than Europe.

Der Polizeipräsident in Berlin
Abteilung II

(Unterschrift der Behörde)

A 5 April 1939

50 RM

Gebühr _____ RM
Geb.-Buch Nr. 335/39/2

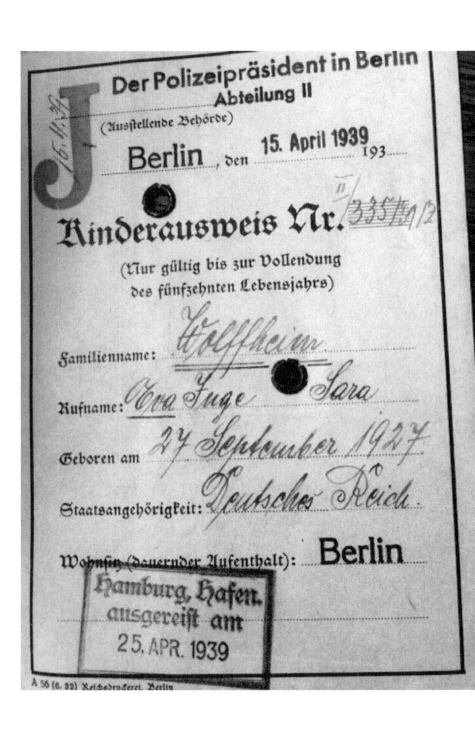

J

Der Polizeipräsident in Berlin
Abteilung II

(Ausstellende Behörde)

Berlin , den 15. April 1939 193

Kinderausweis Nr. II/335/39/12

(Nur gültig bis zur Vollendung
des fünfzehnten Lebensjahrs)

Familienname: Wolffheim

Rufname: Eva Inge Sara

Geboren am 27 September 1927

Staatsangehörigkeit: Deutsches Reich

Wohnsitz (dauernder Aufenthalt): **Berlin**

Hamburg, Hafen.
ausgereist am
25. APR. 1939

A 56 (6. 32) Reichsdruckerei. Berlin

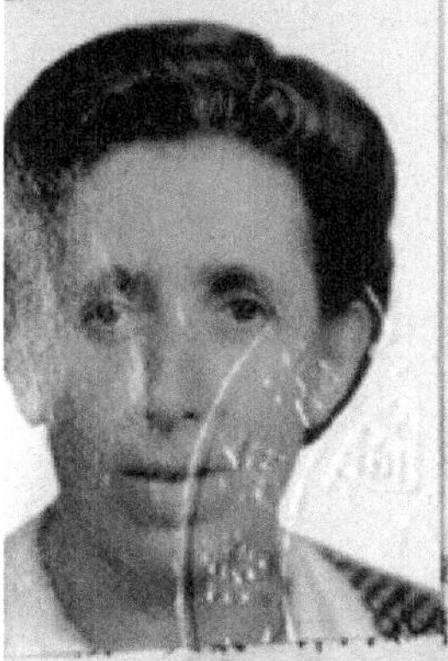

姓名
Name: K. Wolffheim 年齡 Age: JJ 性別 Sex: Female

國籍或籍貫
Nationality or Province: Stateless

shanghai
通訊處
Home Address: 799/3 Tongshan Rd

月，業經全部接種預防疫苗，注射日期 種
下：並經本所加蓋印章，以示慎重。

This is to certify that the above-mentioned person
whose Signature appears below, has been Vaccinated
and Inoculated against the following diseases.

Diseases	注 射 日 期 Date of Inoculation	次 數 No. of Times
黃熱病 Yellow Fever		
鼠疫 Plague		
霍亂 Cholera	1 October 47	1
斑疹傷寒 Typhus Fever		
天花 Smallpox	1 October	1
傷寒 Typhoid Fever		

受種人簽字
Signature of person Vaccinated: Käte Wolffheim

檢疫所蓋印
Official Stamp
of Quarantine
Service

1947

Director

Chapter 7

KAREN

I definitely felt that my mother did not understand me and what it was like to be a child and adolescent in the contemporary world in which I was living. Being the child of immigrants had its challenges, often presenting what I thought were mortifying situations for a young child, preteen, and teenager.

My coats and dresses were purchased longer than what was fashionable, so that I could wear them an extra year or so and then hand them down to my sister, much to her discomfort. I was dressed in sensible clothes not frilly pink dresses and white socks. Thankfully, my mother didn't make me wear brown shoes, which would have been too much. However, I did have leather soled, not rubber soled, saddle shoes until fourth grade, which was humiliating enough. Eventually, as an adult, I felt some gratitude that my mother made sure that my feet and legs were in proper alignment. Almost as bad as the shoes were the embarrassing galoshes we had to wear in the rain and a long raincoat. My mother would question how a short raincoat could protect my clothes from the rain. It was better in my dying-to-conform adolescent mind to have wet feet and clothes and ruin my shoes like everyone else. Go figure. But, such is peer pressure. I never received totally frivolous gifts, such as Barbie dolls, doll clothes and other doll accessories. When I was a preteen, I couldn't get a mohair sweater or the white Go Go boots of the late 1960's. These experiences are indicative of the cultural clashes of immigrants and their American-born offspring and also exemplify generational differences. I never had new pencils only small stubs from who-knows-where. Not only were the pencil erasers non-existent, but I was always looking for a new pencil. It was difficult to do schoolwork with these writing implements. New loose-leaf paper for school was a major luxury.

After we grew too "old" for lunch boxes, my sister Connie and I had to take our daily lunches in used, wrinkled, brown paper bags, not a new fresh one each day. My mother wrapped our liverwurst sandwiches on rye bread together with a cookie to save waxed paper. The cookie was always soggy, with a faint liverwurst flavor. We never had potato chips in our lunch. Today, as an adult, this sounds absurdly inconsequential; but as children my sister and I cringed when we took our lunches out in the cafeteria or schoolyard.

Looking back, these experiences seem laughable; liverwurst on rye bread is a much better sandwich—both in nutrition and taste—than bologna on Wonder Bread, but my sister and I yearned to fit in and be like the others. We wanted to be wasteful like our peers and have pristine pink lunch bags—bought at the supermarket—filled with tasteless white bread sandwiches, devoid of nutrients, cut in quarters with the crusts cut off; potato chips, Hostess cupcakes and neatly cut apple quarters not even turned brown. When we complained, my parents would tell us the story of Leonard, some awful spoiled American boy who wouldn't eat the crust of bread. And his parents condoned such delinquent behavior! If we whined about bread crusts or didn't want to finish our food, my parents always admonished us, "Don't be a Leonard". I never met Leonard, nor do I know the origin of the story. I like to think he's real and that, spoiled though he was, he is a very well-adjusted man who now loves bread crusts and gives all of his leftover food to poor, starving people. When my mother repeated the common expression, used by many parents in the 1950's and 1960's, "Eat your eggs. There are people starving in China." I would answer, "Great. Let's send the eggs to China." It was years later I realized that starvation was a very real threat for my mother in China and learned that she and her compatriots had to scrounge around for enough to eat. Eggs were probably a delicacy, especially if they were fried in butter.

German was never, ever spoken in my home, except by my two grandmothers. I had an interesting conversation with my mother recently regarding this fact. She said, "Our group of friends, both my friends and Dad's, never, ever would have thought to speak German to one another." I asked her why. And she replied, "We hated the Nazis and didn't want to be associated with Germany." As is common among child immigrants, she gave up the language easily when she left Germany at 11 years of age. She had been studying English in Germany and continued to do so in Shanghai.

My parents never purchased German products, such as the popular Volkswagen. My grandmothers, however, couldn't resist some of the German food they were so accustomed to, such as herring, poppy seed pastries and bread, sausages, and chocolates. These delicacies would appear in my grandmothers' apartments and then, somehow, cross the threshold into our home, where they would be gobbled up. I grew up on all-beef, not skinless, hot dogs, with potato salad and rye bread every Sunday night; my parents had beer. The "all-beef" is a concession to my father, who did not like to eat pork.

My family never used Yiddish when I was growing up and to this day, my mother refuses to use colloquial terms, such as "schlepp", "mashuganah", "meshugas", "schlemiel". My father and his mother were a bit more relaxed about not speaking Yiddish. They did say "Good Shabbos" and "Good Yontov", conglomerations of English, Hebrew, and German, the "good" probably derived from "Gut" (good in German). I have picked up Yiddish phrases from living in Boston and Maryland, both areas with many New York and New Jersey transplants who have an Eastern European Jewish background.

A note about Yiddish is in order. Yiddish is primarily a combination of German and Hebrew. Ashkenazi Jews spoke it all over Central and Eastern Europe. In Germany, Yiddish was the primary language of the Jews in Germany until the 17th to 18th centuries. After that time, Yiddish was considered representative of the uneducated or lower classes and was shunned by most German Jews. It was the primary language of women in small religious communities of Eastern Europe, since they were not allowed to speak Hebrew. Since Yiddish was spoken in various countries, Jews could speak a common language when moving around. Yiddish moved with the immigrants to the United States. There is now a strong revival of Yiddish—the language, theater, and literature. Yiddish was originally written with Hebrew characters, so the spelling in English is variable.

Chapter 8

EVA

Approximately, 27,000 Jews left for the United States in 1938 and another 27,000 in 1939. The United States filled its combined German-Austrian quota (which now included annexed Czechoslovakia) for the first time, in 1939. However, this number did not come close to meeting the demand for visas; by June 1939, 309,000 German, Austrian, and Czech Jews had applied for the 27,000 official places available under the U.S. quota. As the poet W.H. Auden so aptly put it:

> *"Saw a poodle in a jacket fastened with a pin,*
> *Saw a door opened and a cat let in:*
> *But they weren't German Jews, my dear, but they weren't*
> *German Jews."*
> From "Refugee Blues", 1939

By early autumn of 1939, approximately 282,000 Jews in total—based on approximately four cumulative years of immigration—had left Germany and 117,000 had migrated from annexed Austria. From this nearly 400,00 total, 95,000 emigrated to the United States, 60,000 to Palestine, 40,000 to Great Britain, and about 75,000 to Central and South America, with the largest numbers going to Argentina, Brazil, Chile, and Bolivia. The Dominican Republic was the only country to increase its quota. More than 18,000 Jews from the German Reich were also able to find refuge in Shanghai, in Japanese-occupied China; a visa was not required for entry into the country. Undoubtedly, there were volumes of paperwork to be completed wherever one attempted to go. The Hilfsverein der Juden in Deutschland, as described earlier, had assisted with plans to travel to China from Germany, though the destination was considered a dangerous and uncertain place as Japan and China were engaged in a war. The Japanese, who were allies of the Nazis, had bombed Chinese cities and massacred inhabitants, most notably in Nanking. Shanghai was considered such a dangerous place that my grandparents didn't take their elderly mothers.

In April of 1939, the family took a train bound to Hamburg, Germany, embarking on their journey from there. The only ships going to Shanghai were Italian, Japanese or German. According to my mother, the family stayed in a nice hotel and said their farewells to the Hamburg branch of my grandfather's family. This included his older brother Alfred, a ship's captain, his Christian wife, and their family. This branch of the family, as mentioned earlier, had converted to Christianity and subsequently survived the war in Germany.

In my mother's memory, the most important part of this story is the farewell dinner my Grandfather Karl hosted. Eva still proudly remembers that everyone "could choose whatever they wanted" from the restaurant menu. She has recounted many times that she ordered "sausage and potato salad" to the adult's chagrin. To this day, this is her favorite meal.

Of course, many details of the departure arrangements are not known, since my mother was 11 years old and not privy to these details—finances, tickets, what was packed and what was left, and other farewells. One detail that my mother remembers is that my grandmother was able to order special furniture for traveling to a new place, which was common in those days.

The ship was the Usaramo, owned and operated by the Deutsche Ost-Afrika-Linie (East Africa Line). It had been launched in 1920, and used as a Reichspostdampfer (mail packet) on the East Africa run and eventually sunk at Bordeaux, France towards the end of the war.

My mother's Uncle Eugen Wolffheim, whose house and business were seized by the Nazis in 1938, also left Germany in May of 1939, an impoverished man. My research shows that Eugen left Berlin for Italy, eventually sailing to Shanghai on the M.V. Terukuni Maru from Naples. Earlier, he and his wife had tried to emigrate to first Bolivia, then Tunisia, and finally the United States, with no luck. Elspeth Wolffheim attempted to follow her husband, but, before she could get her papers in order, tragedy struck. Eugen died of a heart attack in Shanghai. Elspeth lived out her years in Berlin, surviving the prevalent starvation as the war began to falter, the Allied bombing and the Russian atrocities. Weakened by the cruel events of the 30's and 40's, she lived in Berlin until she died in 1951.

As to Eva's two grandmothers, they were left in Berlin in 1939. A few years ago, my mother gave me a small pamphlet called, "The Last Rabbi of Berlin", by Rabbi Bernard M. Zlotowitz, which recounts the story of Rabbi Martin Riesenburger, who was married to a Christian woman, and who remained in Berlin during the war. Rabbi Riesenburger lived in an old-age home and then in the Jewish cemetery. He spent the war years giving his people a Jewish burial, leading services, and ministering to the scattered Jews in Berlin who managed to survive in a horrific situation. Riesenburger endured the war and, with his wife, moved to East Berlin in 1945, and was even able to establish a congregation in East Berlin. According to the story, Martin Riesenburger began as a cantor in pre-war Berlin, and while never ordained a rabbi, performed the functions of one. This story is powerful on several levels; first, his bravery and tremendous faith; second, his "membership" in the small group of men who survived because they were married to Christian women; and third, the old-age home where he worked after 1939 was where my two great grandmothers lived and died, thankfully before the Nazis were able to transport them to Auschwitz. I choose to believe that Rabbi Riesenburger gave both Klara Wolffheim and Rosa Warschauer proper Jewish burials when required. I hope that Rabbi Riesenburger will be long remembered and honored for his courage and fortitude.

Grave of Rosa Warschauer, Berlin.

Sadly, one of the aunties did not fare well. Magda Rosenthal (nee Sandmann) was deported to Theriesenstadt, along with many elderly Jews, and she died in Auschwitz.

The voyage from Hamburg to Shanghai took seventy days. My mother has always told us that she was able to disembark in Lobito, Portuguese West Africa (now Angola), since the ship went around the horn of Africa to get to Asia. According to my mother's eleven-year-old mind, the Wolffheim family members were on a "luxury liner" and were treated to all of the comforts associated with these ships, including activities and elegant meals. More likely, the ship was filled to capacity or over legal limits, considering that the German ship line was making quite a bit of money for the trip to China. My mother has always claimed she had a marvelous time on the boat, but she was 11. We can assume the adults were preoccupied and anxious over what they would find in China and where and how would they live and work.

Chapter 9

KAREN

Like many young American Jews of the time, my sister, Connie and I felt sad that we didn't celebrate Christmas. It was the early to mid-1960s and San Francisco was a very Catholic town. At this time in America, Chanukah was barely acknowledged, not in school, stores, or on television. For a few years, when I was about 12 and Connie was 9, we created our own version, buying candy canes, peppermint gum, making stockings, and cutting down pine boughs for a "Christmas Tree". We exchanged small presents, as well. We were always very happy when Chanukah and Christmas coincided because we had a holiday to celebrate at the same time as everyone else. Our behavior probably comes out of a yearning for assimilation. As an adult, I am glad that our family did not really celebrate Christmas; I feel it would have been "selling-out" on our Jewishness. The drive to blend in was, and remains, very strong. Other racial and ethnic groups did the same and continue to this day. It is difficult to recall now, when the United States Postal Service issues commemorative stamps celebrating not only Chanukah, but Eid al Fit and Chinese New Year, that at one time, quite recently, Americans did not say "Happy Holidays" throughout December, and the Andy Williams Christmas Show was the biggest topic at school the day after it aired.

In my experience, in the United States, especially in years past when Chanukah was essentially ignored and not so widely and broadly celebrated, "having" Christmas was a significant issue for Jews. I know that many American Jewish families actually did celebrate Christmas during this time, to blend in with the mainstream culture. I believe it still is a time of major cultural tension. In my view, the Christmas season is a time when we feel our differentness most intensely, bombarded with Christmas everywhere we go. Aside from the High Holidays and Passover, it is a time when Jews stand alone with different traditions. Until recently, we were the only group that stood out this way. Now, of course, there are many more ethnic and religious groups in this country.

Chanukah celebration, 1957.

I always had ambivalent feelings about being unlike the main-stream group. I feel proud and stand a bit taller when I proclaim that I celebrate a different holiday or have diverse traditions; yet I realize the suffering this religious/ethnic pride has caused through the years. My family witnessed individuals being marched away to unknown fates for belonging to an ethnic group that was blamed for a country's problems. I always feel some-what uneasy, standing alone, like a target. Will someone make a comment? What will I do or say? I will wish "Merry Christmas" to Christians on Christmas, but I feel strange when people wish me the same. Do I go into a lengthy discussion or just nod? Am I gracious or do I get incensed that celebrating Christmas is still an assumption, especially if you don't look "different"? I am responding very much like my mother when she is asked, "Where are you from?" Sometimes she answers truthfully. Other times, she says, "From Europe," and leaves it at that. For young children, it is difficult to realize that a menorah is all we get on Chanukah. Jewish parents can be as joyous as is possible during Chanukah, and we do try, but a menorah is a menorah and not twinkling lights, a colorful tree, brightly wrapped packages, special cookies and candies, and, of course, a jolly bearded man who brings wonderful toys. Even though we did not celebrate Christmas, I was introduced to these traditional holiday foods as a child, and I still enjoy European Christmas goodies during the season.

* * * * *

A recent incident illustrates my parent's efforts at assimilation. This incident also demonstrates how family and individual rituals can come full circle from generation to generation. My mother told me that she celebrated all of the Jewish holidays in Shanghai with joyful events organized by the adults and mentors of the Jewish community, so I know she is aware of traditional Jewish practices for the minor Jewish celebrations.

The phone rang and I ran to pick it up.

"Hello", I said slightly out-of-breath.

"Happy Saint Patrick's Day. I am making corned beef and cabbage", my mother said cheerfully.

I answered matter-of-factly, "Thanks, but I don't celebrate the holiday. I believe that I don't have a bit of Irish in me."

My mother responded, "Oh, I celebrate it. Always have. Your Dad wore a green tie on St. Patrick's Day. And you had to wear green at school, so you wouldn't be pinched. And you played with the Fazackerley girls (friends from our neighborhood, of Irish descent). Now, you and Connie celebrate Purim. I don't. I celebrate St. Patrick's Day."

I commented, "I am sure the corned beef and cabbage will be delicious. I have a confession. I had some Irish Soda Bread ", I said, not wanting to be a spoil-sport.

"Oh, I have that too," my mother said.

* * * * *

The "Christmas" effort was the beginning of the teamwork that characterizes my relationship with my sister. We developed a very tight bond, which continues to this day. When we were children and teenagers, we made every attempt we could to assimilate. Perhaps due to anxiety or just our personalities, we organized our home environment. We cleaned our bedroom and bathroom. We began doing household chores when my mother was very busy with a new baby, my brother, and as well as working part-time. We washed and dried clothes, folded them and put them away. My sister and I ironed too. We wanted clean and pressed clothes. When I was 15 or 16 and my sister was 12 or 13, Connie learned how to sew in Junior High School, and she and I got some money together and she made clothes for us—skirts, tennis dresses, and burlap bags with designs in felt appliqued on the fabric. We shopped together for fabric and both of us had a keen eye for what was stylish. As we got older, we figured out how to get our lunches ready for the next day of school and made our breakfast and got ourselves to school. When I was in High School, my sister and I spent hours discussing the "facts of life" in great depth and detail. Of course, it was a situation of two extremely uninformed young girls doing a great deal of guesswork. Connie and I went on outings together, played tennis, and went shopping—making very careful purchases with our limited funds as we had been taught by example.

We were and are more than sisters; we are friends. I believe our close relationship was fostered by a sense that we had to combine forces to help ourselves learn and adjust to our world, as we experienced it. My sister and I were presented with the challenge of having to show our parents what was typical in our neighborhood in San Francisco in the 1960's. Our childhood and adolescent experiences gave my mother opportunities to learn what was usual in a rather affluent family neighborhood in San Francisco, California, in terms of activities, food, social events, clothing, and education. Our parents were trying to learn the new ways of a new post-War era, country and language. This was especially true for my mother who had arrived ten years later than my father. To this day, my sister and I talk frequently on the phone and discuss how we are different from our mothers and grandmothers and our friends. These are very typical sibling conversations. However, another layer is superimposed on our observations. I am the daughter and granddaughter of women who experienced significant grief, fear, and deprivation over approximately 20 years. My mother and grandmother witnessed events from the horrors of World War II. My mother has told me countless times that she had no idea what American teenagers did and how her American friends had grown up. Her childhood was cut short in Germany. She then went to a ghetto in a war-torn Asian city and survival was a priority. She came to the United States and literally entered a new world.

My parents made certain we were clothed and fed and healthy. My parents raised us not to be spoiled or entitled, all excellent values, which I have come to appreciate even more, as I get older. While I never felt stuffed after meals, there was always enough food on the table. As many immigrants did, my mother shopped every day and only bought enough for the four of us to eat for dinner. Birthdays and vacations were to be cherished and savored as treats or special occasions. Day-to-day existence should not be particularly great or distinctive. How else to distinguish between usual and extraordinary? My mother believes if one suffers just a bit every day, one will deserve the unique enjoyment of exceptional days.

Karen, Connie, and Eva, on Eva's 85th birthday, 2012.

On face value, this does not sound like a particularly bad philosophy, except that it resulted in my aiming for flawlessness in food and experiences, especially on the special days like holidays, birthdays, and vacations. This expectation has always led to distress on my part, since no individual or circumstance is flawless and picture-perfect doesn't exist. I had to learn this lesson through trial and error. But, to this day, in approaching a "special" event, my mother strives for unflawed and impeccable. No glitches, arguments, disappointments, misbehavior, cold food, bad service, or grey skies are to be tolerated on excursions, dinner parties, theater performances, and birthday celebrations. I believe the source of her desire to deprive herself and to strive for sublime perfection on special days is her feeling of guilt at surviving. She may need to withhold pleasure each day in order to feel she deserves to be alive and happy. These idiosyncratic rules about withholding pleasure resulted in my hoarding candy, taking food out of restaurants in napkins to eat later, and saving new clothes for a really special circumstance. My brother, sister, and father also did not wear new clothes immediately. My sister got angry with me for saving my Halloween candy. She always ate hers quickly, probably another reaction to our situation.

The significance of guilt (Survivor's Guilt) to post–World War II victims has been described by both researchers and victims. Primo Levi observed, "That many (including me) experienced 'shame,' that is, a feeling of guilt during the imprisonment and afterward, is an ascertained fact confirmed by numerous testimonies. It is absurd, but it is a fact." Similarly the psychoanalyst Bruno Bettelheim, who was imprisoned in Dachau and Buchenwald in 1938–39, writes: "One cannot survive the concentration camp without feeling guilty that one was so incredibly lucky when millions perished, many of them in front of one's eyes . . . In the camps one was forced, day after day, for years, to watch the destruction of others, feeling—against one's better judgment—

that one should have intervened, feeling guilty for not having done so, and, most of all, feeling guilty for having also felt glad that it was not oneself who perished." In the words of Elie Wiesel, "'I live, therefore I am guilty. I am here because a friend, an acquaintance, an unknown person died in my place'". The survivors of the Shanghai ghetto most probably have experienced another layer of guilt, since they were never subjected to the horrors of the concentration camps in Europe. Not only did they survive the War, but they also did so in the relative safety of a Japanese-controlled ghetto in Asia.

During this time, our family had guests from Germany. Alfred, my grandfather's brother, had a daughter, Kaethe, who was a teenager during World War II. I met Kaethe in the 1960's and I have spent a little time with her daughter, Susann, over the years. Susann was born in 1945. In 1961, she visited us in San Francisco. I visited her in Hamburg in 1973 and again in Berlin in 2014. She has visited my mother in San Francisco on several occasions. They share a love for opera. Our dear family friends, the Sumners, visited us in the summer of 1962. Ruth and Forest Sumner (Shanghai) had two children and we had a great time together.

Our family attended Temple Emanuel in San Francisco. Temple Emanuel is a beautiful San Francisco landmark, with its Moorish style architecture and large dome, visible from many high places in the city. The synagogue had a Reform affiliation and was very similar to the large temples my mother attended in Berlin. She was comfortable in this environment and somehow she convinced my father to join. He would have preferred the smaller Conservative Temple Beth Shalom, where my parents were married.

Chapter 10

EVA

The Usaramo arrived in Shanghai on June 29, 1939 by way of the Whangpoo River. From what I have learned, their first views of China were not picturesque gardens and traditional buildings but flat farmland, power plants, smelly wharves and decrepit warehouses.

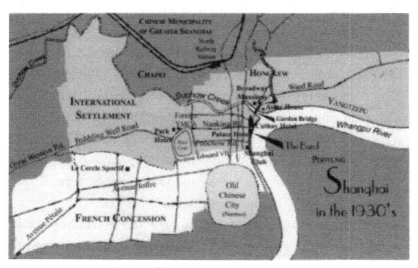

Map of Shanghai in the 1930s.

When my mother's family arrived, Shanghai was a wild, un- ruly cosmopolitan city, filled with crooks of all ages and types, criminal gangs, small-time petty thieves as well as war-time "en- trepreneurs" and adventurers of various sorts. Supposedly, at this time there were more prostitutes per capita than in any other city in the world. These women ranged from high class courtesans in villas to lower class prostitutes in opium dens. Sadly, some destitute Jewish women also had to resort to pros- titution in the 1940's. Pickpockets and beggars were organized into professional groups, and powerful gangs controlled large sections of legitimate Shanghai. There were still huge discrep- ancies between rich and poor and men and women. Wealthy Chinese snubbed the lower classes and foreigners, and the Eu- ropeans looked down upon all of the Chinese. However, when it came to doing business, everyone was willing to put on a good face and commerce was lucrative for entrepreneurs of all levels and types. The free-for-all atmosphere was due to the constant power struggles in Shanghai and lack of strong and steady gov- ernmental control. Unfortunately, the chaos continued until the Communist Revolution.

My mother's view of humankind was negatively affected by her early experiences in Shanghai. The more affluent Chinese placed little value on the lives of the poor Chinese. The Japanese placed no value at all on the lives of the Chinese, in general, but were ambivalent about the Jews. She already had an idea what Nazis were capable of and now she saw Japanese kick Chinese people to the ground and worse and the Japanese were the au- thorities she and her family now had to live under.

My mother has told me that on arrival, she and her family were taken by open truck to a processing center and then to some temporary shelter, a far cry from the comfortable flats of Berlin. Jewish Shanghailanders were there to assist them.

(Shanghai Chinese were referred to as Shanghainese and foreigners were known as Shanghailanders.) There are many pictures from this time of overdressed German and Austrian men and women and their families, being assisted by Chinese laborers in rags. The immigrants would have been assaulted by the stench of the wharf and the oppressive humidity of June, since Shanghai has a climate similar to Washington D.C. or Atlanta, Georgia. The recent arrivals would also have their first exposure to the unfamiliar sound and rhythms of the Chinese language, coming from dockworkers and peddlers and their customers on the crowded streets. This must surely have added to a sense of extreme chaos.

My mother does not remember much of the very early period of adjustment in Shanghai. She has said that following a short stay in a temporary shelter of some kind, they moved to an apartment on Ford Road in the International Settlement. Eva's urbane and well-traveled Uncle Eugen and cousin Hans Mayer lived in the French Concession who they visited. After the attack on Pearl Harbor, my mother and her family had to move to another part of the International Settlement, in an area known as Hong Kou or Hongkew.

For the most part, the refugees set up a community that was based on self- and mutual- support. Families lived together in apartments or flats in low-rise brick buildings, which were arranged in the Chinese style of square blocks, separated by a maze of lanes. Only a few of the apartment houses faced the main street. The lanes were important places for the Chinese and Europeans. In summer, children played while the European adults cooked and socialized in the narrow alleyways. As ugly as they were, the buildings were far better than those of the working Chinese. And some of the less fortunate or able Europeans had to live in Heime (German for homes) that were actually crowded dormitories with poor sanitary conditions.

Maze of lanes in modern-day Hong Kou.

The apartment houses where the Wolffheims lived consisted of two to three floors, a family per floor or two families
on each floor. There were primitive outhouses and indoor and
outdoor makeshift kitchens. In summer, it was extremely hot,
so, as much as possible, life was conducted outdoors. In winter,
it was damp and cold, so most people spent their time at home

in bed, under the blankets, wearing their clothing. During the rainy season, the sewers overflowed, and raw sewage spilled over into the streets. Rats, lice and other vermin were a constant presence. According to my mother's friend, Fred Cohn, also a Shanghai refugee, the three families that lived in the building on Tongshan Road, which was to be her second residence in Shanghai, purchased the property.

Apartment on Tongshan Road.

People had dysentery from the water and fruits and vegetables, and they had all sorts of parasites from the meat, including trichinosis. Food was scarce and meals consisted of beans, potatoes, a little meat, and few vegetables and fruits, always boiled. Milk had to be boiled; butter was a delicacy. Upper respiratory infections were common from the damp and cold and people frequently were very ill and/or died from typhus and other deadly diseases, due to their poor immunity caused by a lack of proper nutrition. Many of my mother's compatriots had chronic health conditions while living in Shanghai and afterwards in the United States—circulation, skin, and digestive problems, to name a few. And, of course, these people could be considered the lucky ones. Many, many Jews succumbed to illnesses in Shanghai brought on by living in a densely populated area, with horrendous public health dangers. Children were often left without parents, due to death from disease, and were informally adopted by other families. Such was the case with my mother's friend Fred Cohn and his sister. However, the children were separated, with Fred going to one family and his sister to another. Fred's sister was "adopted" by a Hungarian doctor and his wife. The doctor was able to nurse his sister back to health, from typhus. Fred was "adopted" by Siegfried and Nellie Cohn who lived in the same building as my mother.

Fred Cohn and Eva, September 27, 2015, her 88th birthday.

Tragically, Gunther, my mother's older brother, died in 1940 of pneumonia, a complication of his chronic asthma. I know that this was a severe blow to my grandmother. I do not think she ever recovered from this loss. She had spent a great deal of energy in Germany, helping her son in any way possible. To lose him, in a strange land, completely devoid of what she knew was healthy for him, must have been a cruel blow.

Most of the Jews in Shanghai (and in Germany previously) were practical, always adjusting, coping and learning new skills. Such were the characteristics of these German and Austrian Jews who left their comfortable lives to attempt to survive in a strange land. The women and men went to work, setting up retail and wholesale businesses. A laundry, shoe repair shop, tailor, bakery, grocer, and pharmacy were required. Since most of the refugees were from Germany and Austria, cafes serving coffee and pastries were opened rather soon after the immigrants arrived. There is always time for the obligatory "Café und Kuchen", coffee and cake. There were also butcher shops with sausages. How the refugees obtained the ingredients for these treats is a mystery to me; but Shanghai was a city where just about anything could be obtained for a price. The streets in Hongkew began to resemble streets in Europe. Some of the doctors and lawyers practiced, as did the other medical workers. My grandfather sold various items, as a distributor of sorts. My grandmother was a nurse and social worker. While licenses were not required in the free-for-all environment of Shanghai, the refugees had all been well-trained in Europe.

The Jewish people have been accustomed to moving around throughout history, so they have the coping skills necessary to rebuild a civilized life wherever they find themselves, and Shanghai was no exception. There were some Jewish organizations prior to the influx of World War II refugees. There were already Jews in Shanghai and, as a result, the Jewish burial society—

Chevra Kadisha— the Hebrew Relief Society, the Jewish Education Society, Bnai Brith, Council of Jewish Women, and various Zionist groups were already in place. The members of these organizations—primarily Sephardic and Russian Jews— attempted to help the influx of refugees in 1939. Of course, they were overwhelmed, and new groups were established, such as the International Committee for the Organization of European Immigrants in China (IC) and the Committee for the Assistance of European Refugees in Shanghai (CFA). The Jewish Gemeinde (Jewish Communal Association) was formed and set up a democratic government of sorts. The Gemeinde coordinated religious, educational, legal, and economic functions.

Present day Shanghai, formerly area of
Jewish shops in Hongkew (Hong Kou).

My mother has never mentioned these groups, but she wouldn't have been concerned with this aspect of life as she was now becoming a teenager. Perhaps, my grandmother worked for one of these groups. How the people who worked at the social service agencies were paid is a mystery, though there was a little money coming in from the U.S.A. and England prior to the onset of the war.

There were some wealthy, established, Middle Eastern Jews who had been doing business in China for a long time. These Middle Eastern Sephardi Jews were mostly from Iraq, which was a British colony at the time. These Sephardim helped a great deal with schools, medical facilities and recreational activities. However, when Japan entered the war, they were collected and sent to the prison camps, as they held British passports and were now considered enemies. There were also some West European Ashkenazi Jews in Shanghai that had been there after escaping from Russia and they were more inclined to help the Polish Jews who came in the late summer of 1941. Quakers and Christian missionaries also helped the destitute Jewish refugees.

The Chinese have always "looked the other way" when it comes to the Jews, up to the present day. For example, there is an ancient city in China, Kaifeng, where a small community of practicing Jews has lived for centuries. It is believed that they are descendants of Sephardi Jews who came to the region for purposes of commerce. Amazing as it seems, the Chinese have allowed the Jews of Kaifeng to continue to quietly practice their religion and customs. The Jews did not proselytize as the Christian missionaries did, so perhaps, an animosity never developed between the Chinese and the Jews. I like to believe that the Jews and Chinese found a commonality in values, for example, love of learning, business acumen, and a veneration of ancestors. The Chinese have ventured past their borders to do business and search for a better life, as the Jews have been forced to do over the centuries. So perhaps there is a mutual respect. Regardless, the Chinese did not bother the Jews in Shanghai prior to the World Wars and in the 1940's, and the Jewish people were welcome until the Communist Revolution.

Residents of "lane" in 2007, adjacent to Tongshan Road, site of Eva's apartment. These women said they had lived there all of their lives. My mother never played with Chinese girls.

Before the Sino/Japanese War, there were also vibrant Jewish communities in Manchuria. These Jews were primarily Russian and went to that harsh land as a result of Tsar Nicholas II's plan to "Russify" the area. The largest community of Jews was in Harbin, with smaller groups in towns such as Darien. Jews were primarily engaged in commerce. When the Japanese took over the area in 1931, the relatively peaceful coexistence turned ugly. The Japanese ganged up with the anti-Semitic White Russians and there was grave trouble for the Jews, with most of them leaving for Shanghai or other Chinese cities.

Less known is the relationship between the Japanese and the Jews. Based on the book, *The Fugu Plan*, an interesting story emerges concerning the Japanese and the Jews of Asia. In the fall of 1939, after the Nazi invasion of Poland, a Dutch ambassador, L.P.J. de Dekker, decided to allow his consulates throughout Eastern Europe to issue stamps on the passports of refugees which stated: "No visa to Curacao is required." The strategy was that this stamp might allow the Jewish refugees to travel safely through the Soviet Union, ostensibly on their way to Curacao, which was a Dutch colony at the time. Many Jews were concentrated in the Baltic state of Lithuania and for whatever reason, the Japanese Consul in Kovno, Lithuania, Chuine Sugihara felt a moral obligation to help these Jews, who had escaped Poland ahead of the Nazis, and would either be killed by invading Nazis or sent to Siberia by the Russians. Consul Sugihara decided to issue any refugee with the Dutch stamp that noted a destination of Curacao, transit visas for travel through Japan and a temporary stay in the country. Consul Sugihara issued these visas in August of 1940 and was dismissed from Kovno in September of 1940. He had acted independently and in defiance of what the Japanese authorities had clearly forbidden. Thanks to his actions and those of Ambassador de Dekker, several thousand Polish Jews, including the students and teachers of the famous Mir Yeshiva, were saved and allowed to travel through Russia to Kobe, Japan. The Jews made a temporary home for themselves in Kobe, which was a temperate, pleasant seaside town. However, there was no way they would be allowed in the United States, Great Britain, or Australia due to immigration quotas and restrictions. While the Curacao stamp had been a ruse, some Jews did manage to get to South America during the late 1930's and 1940's.

Simultaneous to Consul Sugihara and Ambassador de Dekker's humanitarian efforts, high level Japanese governmental officials had secretly developed a plan to settle European Jews in some area of Japanese-held Asia, possibly Manchukuo (Manchuria). It was secretly referred to as the "Fugu Plan". The name of the plan reflects the ambivalence the Japanese felt for the Jews. The fugu is a very poisonous blowfish. After the toxin-containing organs are removed, the fish is eaten. The fugu is thought to be a rare delicacy. If the fish is not prepared in the correct manner, its poison will kill anyone who eats it.

The true motive behind the "Fugu Plan" was, that by saving the Jews, the Japanese would receive accolades from the United States and perhaps receive money from wealthy Jews, such as the Rothschild's. The United States had already established an embargo severely hampering trade for Japan and the Japanese believed that if the Americans saw how "good" the Japanese were in their treatment of the Jews, they might change their minds about the embargo. Also, the Japanese had the misguided belief, probably gleaned from German propaganda, that Jews not only controlled President Roosevelt but also could influence world commerce and economics. Some Japanese firmly believed that Roosevelt was Jewish. Rabbi Stephen Wise, an American rabbi, rejected any overtures by Japan to benefit Jews or anyone else. He believed that the Japanese were only attempting to save their reputation not reveal their true motives.

When the Japanese signed the Tripartite Agreement with Germany and Italy in September of 1940, the Nazis put pressure on Japan to "do something" with the Jews and, as a result, the Jews who had immigrated to Kobe went to Shanghai in 1941, where the Shanghai Ashkenazi Relief Association (SACRA) took responsibility for assisting them. That was the end of the "Fugu Plan".

My mother has never mentioned anything about "new" Jews arriving in 1941, but, of course, she was 14. She was more interested in the typical adolescent activities rather than the very different Polish Jews. This was a group of Jews from Eastern Europe.

A final word about the Japanese treatment of Jews in Japan prior to the Pearl Harbor attack. While individuals in official circles in Japan were known to be anti-Semitic, they didn't hate

Jews because they were Jews, but rather they feared their "different-ness" and associated Jews with both or either Communism and simultaneously Capitalism, based on the bizarre theory of Jewish control of world finances. Although the Japanese treated the Jews humanely in their own country, they became brutal when they were the aggressors, for example in China. The Japanese were shrewd and wanted to use the Jews to their advantage, both in Japan and in Shanghai. To this day, there is a Jewish community in Tokyo. When all is said and done, the Japanese did not undertake to exterminate the Jews and actually hid some influential Jews in the interior of Japan throughout World War II.

Recently, I discovered that the Chinese Consul in Vienna during this time, Ho Feng Shan, issued approximately 10,000 visas to Jews for purposes of travel to Shanghai, to escape the Nazis. This in itself was a heroic act, but he also defied his superiors in signing off on thousands of unauthorized visas. However, since visas were not necessary to enter Shanghai, the greater purpose in his actions was to alert the thousands of Jews in surrounding countries, especially Germany, that Shanghai was a viable destination once they escaped Nazi control. Some refugees were able to use the visas to travel to other countries, for example the United States and the Philippines. Ho Feng Shan is now known as the "Chinese Schindler". He lived in San Francisco after the war and never told anyone about his actions. His daughter discovered this surprising information when she was conducting research for a book about her father. How ironic that this kind man was living in the same city as my mother. Of course, she never knew him, the man possibly responsible for her father's decision to escape to Shanghai.

The children were sent to school very soon after the refugees arrived in Shanghai. School, then as now, probably was one of the most important aspects of life for the children and adolescents. Some sort of normalcy returned to their lives with minds and bodies occupied with appropriate activities. My mother has freely shared stories about her school life in Shanghai. At first, my mother attended a school run by missionaries, which Eva called the "Bible School." She said that she enjoyed the school because the students "read from the bible, sang songs, played in the church pews, and ate cookies." Soon, however, members of the Jewish community complained to my grandparents that they were "concerned" about Eva attending a Christian school, so she transferred to the Kadoorie School. Eva was interviewed for admission by Mrs. Lucie Hartwich, a former teacher in Germany, and now Headmistress at the school. My mother recounted that as her English language skills were strong, she entered the Jewish school at a "high level." Throughout my childhood, my mother regaled my siblings and me with stories of school. She told us countless tales about Mrs. Christiansen, a strict teacher that the students were not fond of, and who, perhaps because of this, referred to her students as "hooligans". We heard about my mother's friends, male and female, and her favorite classes, which certainly did not include mathematics (like me). She was a much stronger student in high school than she had been in primary school. She can still remember the class officers, the scholars, and the athletes. To this day, if I mention someone, she will say, "Oh, he was class president. Oh, he was a brain. Oh, he was a class clown."

Michael Blumenthal, Secretary of the Treasury in the Carter administration, lived in Shanghai. He was not a personal friend of my mother's, since he attended a different school and was a year older. Some of the adolescents who came to Shanghai in their late teens had a more difficult time than the younger ones who were in their early adolescent years. These "older" students did not have the protection of school after their mid-teens and had to search for work in an environment of unemployment, inflation, and general chaos. She recalled the extracurricular groups and activities such as field trips, athletics and hikes. The curriculum was British, so my mother learned a British English. She said that she sounded English when she arrived in the United States, eventually losing the accent. She also learned English customs, such as teatime, and studied English history and literature. Before 1942, there was still a bit of money and time to visit the Cathay Hotel—now the Peace Hotel—to have an ice cream, pastry, lemonade, or coffee and listen to some Viennese music, perhaps a Strauss waltz. And a Sunday afternoon offered time to walk along The Bund, a famous wide avenue along the Whangpoo River. The Bund is famous for its tall buildings, massive banks, lavish hotels, and traditional clubs. This was a European façade for a decidedly Chinese city of narrow streets, alleys, and lanes, crowded with people of all sorts, from "coolies" to Chinese women hobbling on bound feet to men with long braids quickly walking to some important destination.

The Kadoorie School was named after the Kadoories, a wealthy Iraqi Jewish family who had come to Shanghai around 1870 from Baghdad via India, eventually becoming British citizens. Sir Victor Sassoon was considered the leader of this group of Jews, which also included the Hayims, the Abrahams, and the Hardoons. My mother always spoke fondly of these benefactors. Horace Kadoorie established the Shanghai Jewish Youth Association (S.J.Y.A.) in 1937, which consisted of summer camps, athletic events, and film and theater productions. After the influx of Jewish refugees in 1939, the S.J.Y.A assisted the Shanghai Jewish School (S.J.S.) in expanding to cope with the huge increase in numbers of students, and it eventually became known as the Kadoorie School. My mother recently told me that she met Sir Victor Sassoon in San Francisco when he was 90 years old.

Eva as a Girl Guide in 1941, approximately.

Eva has told me that she received a well-rounded education while living in Shanghai but never mastered the Chinese language. She has said, "I knew a few phrases in Chinese. When I lived there, it was still a very international city, so you could exist in your own community without having to learn the language."

Now I tell the story of the three friends, Eva, Ruth, and Inge. Eva is my mother. My mother became friends with Ruth and Inge in Shanghai when she was a young teenager, maybe 13. My mother had lost another friend, also named Ruth, to a tragedy. The first Ruth died of a ruptured appendix in Shanghai at the age of 12. Of course, this should have never happened, but it appears that the symptoms of appendicitis were confused with those of dysentery. This was a huge loss to my mother. When she tells the story, I can still feel the tragic and shocking loss. They had been friends in Berlin as little girls. Ruth's parents, Edith and Werner Falk, were my grandparents' best friends and lived very close in Shanghai. I met them on several occasions, and the sense of loss and tragedy infused their personas.

Ruth (the second, Shanghai friend) and Inge were my mother's closest girlfriends through her teenage and young adult years. Both girls were from the eastern part of Germany, with Inge from Neurode in Silesia, and Ruth from Beaton in a coal mining area. All three were born in the fall of 1927 and, once they met in China, seem to have been inseparable until the end of the war. Even today these women (including my mother) are alive and in touch with each other. Ruth lives in Florida and Inge and Eva live in California. My mother describes a great deal of freedom, with the three of them wandering around the International Settlement, eating sunflower seeds and endlessly talking about boys and movies. Even though Shanghai was a crime-ridden city, schoolgirls did not appear to be in danger, according to my mother. They walked to school, were out at night, and went to extracurricular activities and social events, such as hayrides, campfires, beach trips, dances, and parties. I can visualize the three girls walking with arms looped together passing bars and brothels, filled with soldiers, first American, then Japanese, then American again.

Inge, Eva, Ruth 2000.

Most probably, their parents were so concentrated on survival, that they had no energy left to monitor their children. This was probably a blessing in disguise as my mother has always described this time in her life as a great adventure, a time of carefree fun. It is true that the teachers and youth leaders attempted to create a safe and positive environment for the young people, and the Jewish holidays were observed and activities appropriate to the celebrations occurred.

However, all of this "fun", a word that I heard frequently in connection to China as I grew up, must have been foreshadowed by death, illness, loss, grief, and confusion. I believe both experiences were occurring simultaneously for my mother and her peers. It has been documented by my mother and other survivors that the young people were able to go on excursions to areas outside of Shanghai, until the bombing by the allies began and then after the war. These were young people who were determined to live in the present and enjoy what was possible in a dangerous environment. They were a close, tight knit group with a great deal in common and they bonded. Their friendships endure to the present, forged by tragedy and fear, much as soldiers become close buddies in war.

Eva, on one of her adventures in China.

Chapter 11

KAREN

From my perspective, as a child and teenager living in San Francisco in the 1960's, the book and movie, "Exodus", finally brought me some much-needed clarity into what had been for me the closed chapters of the story of European Jews from 1933-45. I devoured the book, unable to put the book down, and felt every detail as if I was experiencing it personally. At this same time, I read *The Diary of Anne Frank*, saw the movie and was, of course, deeply affected.

My parents could not answer my most pressing questions, such as "How could this happen?", and "If there is a God, how would he let innocent people be killed?" My father asked the same questions, and my mother remained silent. I remember sitting in the kitchen for hours, listening to my parents speak about their pasts. Actually, my father spoke while my mother listened. With the exception of the loss of his mother, at the age of four, my father described an idyllic childhood in southern Germany, The paternal grandmother I adored was actually my father's "stepmother", his father's second wife. My father spoke of cousins and summers in the country. He also spoke of ending school after his Bar Mitzvah and abruptly being sent to an apprenticeship program for bakers which he hated because he was treated badly. Vocational training was quite popular in the late 1930's among German and Austrian Jews, as they began to see "the handwriting on the wall" and sent their children and themselves to training schools. They were preparing to leave the country.

My paternal grandmother also shared her stories. I listened to their narratives with fascination, glued to my chair. She was from a very affluent family, near Frankfurt, and went to boarding school and art school. She told me stories about helping a Jewish family escape via Switzerland, lifelong friends from her childhood who she would later meet again in the United States, of having an adoring father, and a very difficult mother.

I began to form vivid pictures in my mind of the people and places they described—a paper cone filled with candies, wild berry juice, buttery cakes, walking arm-in-arm with father, broken skis, hot milk, the death of a parent, unbearable heat and bone chattering cold, a sick brother and a worried mother, jewels sewn in jackets, and leather money pouches around one's neck. And most definitely, I perceived an overall sense of anxiety and mistrust being clearly communicated to me. There were some "good Germans" but most had turned against my family members. There was danger around every corner and always the threat that something would go terribly wrong and tragedy would strike.

On the other hand, my maternal grandmother, Kaethe, rarely spoke of Shanghai and Germany. I think that these subjects were just too painful for her, and her English was not as fluent as my other grandmother's.

Omi Kaethe, around 1968.

I clearly remember attending my first political demonstration in San Francisco. The rally was for freeing Russian Jews and it was held in Sigmund Stern Grove, a eucalyptus grove that is almost like a rain forest. The area is usually cold and wet. The dancing and singing and shouting exhilarated me. I expected my mother to be proud of me; however, she was fearful and negative and very disdainful of the demonstration. She said that crowds were dangerous. I did not feel validated at a time when I was seeking parental approval. However, now I realize her fear comes from the days in Berlin when she witnessed the large Nazi rallies.

Karen and Connie, 1966, approximately.

My life was filled with reminders of the past, which was, I believe, a different experience from most teenagers of my generation. On a Sunday afternoon and on Jewish holidays, I encountered my Grandmother Kaethe's friends. I remember going to their apartments and having cake or sweets and being admired just because I was a granddaughter. My sister and I goofed around and played outside, while the adults conversed in German. I remember my grandmother's friends who had also lived in Shanghai—intelligent and funny Mrs. Frankel; sweet and fragile Mrs. Buchstab; Mrs. Weil and her son: Mrs. Shaie and her son and daughter, Anita and Jerry; and Dr. Schnitkin, who played the recorder. I even met Mrs. Hartwich, the former teacher and headmistress, at the Jewish Home of San Francisco, on Silver Avenue, in the late 1960's. I remember a cheery elderly lady who was thrilled to see my mother again.

Some Holocaust survivors, my maternal grandmother, Omi Kaethe, for example, did not fare well emotionally. I knew inherently that she was fragile and that I had to tread very carefully with her, being sure not to say anything that would hurt her feelings. She could change unpredictably from happy to sad in a very short time. Later I learned that my Grandmother Kaethe suffered from severe depression and possibly bipolar disorder from the 1950's to the early 1970's. It is possible that the illness was brought on by the trauma she suffered in Shanghai. As I remember my grandmother, the loss of her son and husband lingered about her. I have vivid memories of a generous, altruistic, funny woman who was extremely emotional. She had no patience for most conventions and was devoted to my mother and me and my sister and brother. My grandmother Kaethe had many friends and was very social. I believe she was easily hurt by others. Sometimes, she literally went from laughing to crying within minutes. I was too young to have clear memories of her for most of the 1950's, and she died in 1974. I have definitely inherited some of her emotional sensitivity and passion and devotion to the less fortunate.

Eva's brother, Gunther, age 18, Shanghai.

It is no wonder that the former Shanghailanders my siblings and I met in the 1950's-1970's seemed fragile to us or strange in any number of ways. And now, looking back, each one of those brave men and women had stories that would make anyone deeply shocked and saddened.

My sister and brother and I grew up socializing with other Shanghai-survivor families. These were my mother's friends and one relative who lived in the San Francisco Bay Area and one family in Florida. I remember numerous Sunday afternoons, visiting—or being visited by—these families and playing with the kids for endless hours. The pattern was always the same. We arrived at the house of our friends, usually in the suburbs, and sat down for "Kaffee und Kuchen". Then we kids played. We were just youngsters playing indoors and outside, unaware of any special bond. I remember hide and seek, riding on the handlebars of a bicycle, and putting on plays, sometimes with Jewish and/or biblical themes. Then it was time for dinner and a drowsy ride back to the city.

Karen, Connie, and Inge's two oldest children, 1958, approximately.

Levi family and Sumner family (Ruth and Forrest), 1968.

Chapter 12

EVA

In November 1941, the German Consul General informed the Jews of Shanghai that they had lost their German citizenship and that "the assets of a Jew, who according to this proclamation loses his citizenship, are taken over by the Third Reich." This came as no surprise, and the Shanghailanders no longer cared any more if they were German citizens. And, at this point, they didn't really have any assets.

On December 7, 1941, the same day that the Japanese attacked Pearl Harbor, they bombed Shanghai harbor. Reportedly my mother "slept through" this attack, thus validating her ability and reputation to "sleep through anything".

After 1941, when the war in the Pacific began, there was a news blackout with the Japanese controlling the International Settlement and being cut off from the world must have been agony for everyone.

According to my mother, from 1942 on, the Japanese made life even more miserable and precarious for the now stateless Jews, now lacking consular protections. The rights of the Jews were slowly eroded as the war in the Pacific proceeded. They were imprisoned for "spying"; their radios were confiscated and the self-governing body was dissolved. In February 1943, the Jews were ordered to live and work in a small area of the International Settlement known as Hongkew (Hong Kou). My mother and her family moved to a flat on Tongshan Road. So an already crowded place became more cramped and less habitable. The Japanese continued to make a bad situation worse. By this time, the British had already been put in POW camps, a situation depicted in the book by J.G. Ballard, and later a Steven Spielberg movie, "Empire of the Sun". The Russian and Middle Eastern Jews were allowed to continue to live in better parts of Shanghai, as they were not considered enemies of the Axis powers. The Kadoorie School was closed and a new school opened in the area where the Jews were allowed to live. My mother was 15 at this point and the school authorities decided that students of this age were finished with school. As a result my mother went on to a business school to learn shorthand, typing, and book-keeping.

Misery was everywhere. My mother has reported that she stepped over dead Chinese, who had starved or frozen to death, every morning on her way to school. She recounted a harrowing tale from her own experience. She had become deathly ill from typhus and was bundled onto a stretcher and rushed, being carried by young Chinese men, as there were no ambulances, to the hospital, with my Grandmother Kaethe running behind, screaming and yelling, fearful she would lose another child. My mother's peers frequently lost parents to disease and were informally adopted by caring neighbors. Children succumbed to diseases that would have been treatable in a more developed country.

At 17 my mother began to work and receive advanced professional training, so she had a special pass to leave the restricted area. A Japanese bureaucrat by the name of Ghoya was the dreaded individual who dispensed these I.D. cards. According to various accounts, Ghoya was a short man—even for Japanese standards—who acted erratically and violently to Jews attempting to renew their work passes. He told people that he was "The King of Jews".

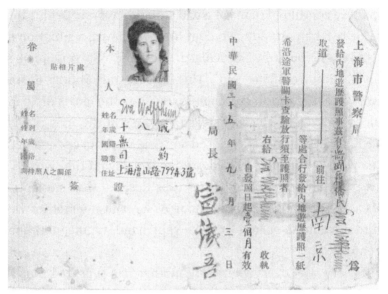

Eva's I.D. card to leave Hongkew (Hong Kou), 1942.

My mother has told me that the Japanese were "almost as bad to the Chinese as the Nazis were to the Jews." She witnessed Japanese soldiers kicking innocent Chinese and signs barring the Chinese from public places appeared. For the Jews, this must have been a shocking reminder of the Nazis and the fragility and precariousness of life. To this day, my mother can recognize the physical differences between a Japanese, a Chinese, and a Korean person immediately, an uncanny skill for a Caucasian and one I have only slightly mastered. It was a matter of survival on the streets of Shanghai to know if you were approaching a hostile Japanese soldier or a non-hostile Chinese man.

At some point during this period, my mother became an apprentice in a laboratory in the Ward Road Camp hospital. Ward Road was a camp for Jewish immigrants who didn't have sufficient funds to buy or share an apartment. She was trained to be a "lab technician" or "laboratory technologist", as it was called in those days. She told me that she worked with a Hungarian doctor who was "very helpful" in her training. According to a report written by a historian from Hungary, the doctor was a Hungarian physician by the name of Dr. Veroe, a Jewish refugee himself. Due to the poor sanitary conditions in Shanghai overall, but especially in the refugee camps, dysentery and parasites were common. Eva tested blood, urine and fecal samples. When we were children, my mother used to thrill (or disgust) us with stories about arduously looking for the head of a tapeworm in a stool sample; unless the head was found, the tapeworm could not be eradicated from the patient's body.

She took her training and skills in laboratory technology with her to the United States and later worked in labs as I was growing up. Eva learned to draw blood, and analyze the blood, using the techniques of the day. I remember watching her when I was about nine years old, peering through the microscope and counting blood cells with a counter (like a clicker). She was meticulous and careful, so she was probably very good at drawing blood. My mother was precise to a fault, so she was most probably excellent in the techniques for blood analysis that were the standard for the day.

Due to the ceaseless work of Laura Margulies of the Jewish Distribution Committee (JDC) and cooperation from the U.S. Treasury and State Departments and the American Red Cross , Mrs. Margulies was able to obtain funds and food for the Jewish refugees in Shanghai.

Site of the American Jewish Joint Distribution Committee.

After Pearl Harbor, it became increasingly difficult to transfer money and supplies to Shanghai. The U.S. government ultimately refused to cooperate in sending anything to Shanghai because it was under Japanese control. The situation became more and more desperate among all residents, since the war had eliminated most business dealings. By 1944 even trading in the Japanese-controlled areas had ceased, since the Allies were making headway in the Pacific theatre. Locally, the Japanese further restricted the issue of passes to the residents of Hongkew, thereby preventing them from working in other sections of Shanghai.

Chinese paper currency, period unknown.

The winter of 1943-44 was the coldest on record for Shanghai in twenty years and residents of the International Settlement did not have money to buy proper clothing, food, and blankets. Coal for heating had disappeared and electricity was rationed. Unemployment created more tension and desperation, especially among the men. Inflation was exorbitant. By 1944, the Shanghai dollar was valued down to a hundred per one U.S. dollar and dropping continuously. By 1945, the value was down to one hundred thousand to one U.S. dollar. By mother tells of people using a wheelbarrow, full of paper money, to shop for groceries.

Chapter 13

KAREN

As a young adult, I felt intrigued about my parents' stories and I was excited to learn more. Studying American and European history, it became evident that the few adventures my mother had related were just the tip of the iceberg. I became Zionistic and learned Hebrew and took up Israeli folk dancing. Acutely aware of the Palestinian and Israeli problems, I was very conflicted about the situation. I asked questions but then answered them quickly myself. I did not want to question my allegiance to Israel. And I couldn't tolerate thinking about Israel in a less positive way. I visited both Germany and Israel in 1973 and was deeply affected by my experiences in both countries.

I also developed an avid interest in all things Asian; a fascination helped by the fact that I lived in San Francisco and went to Chinatown frequently. I also went to a high school in the mid to late 1960's with many Chinese students. This was the beginning for me of my interest in the China—Jewish connection. For me, this curiosity is a combination of being Jewish, a natural affinity for all things Asian, and an abiding interest in what had occurred to my mother and her compatriots in China. I have followed this complex and enriching interest since then.

At the beginning of college, I declared a major in German,

since studying foreign languages was an area of study I truly enjoyed. However, I soon realized that my feelings about Germans and Germany caused me severe discomfort. Therefore, I changed my major and graduated with a B.A. in Speech and Hearing from University of California at Santa Barbara in 1973, and obtained my M.A. in Communicative Disorders from Emerson College in Boston in 1976. My career as a practicing Speech/Language Pathologist lasted 36 years, until my retirement in 2012. The person I am today is in part due to my experiences working with children and educational staff in Montgomery County Public Schools. My perspective on life has been influenced by working in a busy, ever-changing suburban/urban school district. I have come in contact with people from all over the world of diverse socio-economic levels. What I gave and received in my career helped me to become a better person and mother.

The survival skills my mother developed in Shanghai became the basis for values instilled in me as I grew up. Yes, by all means, education comes first; however, don't forget to be prepared to earn money in a good job, so you can support yourself (and your family). And for that reason, I chose a college major that lead to a specific job (by way of a Master's degree, as well). I knew I wanted to be in a helping profession from an early age, so my decision to become a Speech Pathologist accomplished both goals, practicality and working with people to better their lives.

College and graduate school were years of self-absorption and preparation for adult life, and I did not concern myself too much with my parents and their backgrounds. Leaving home to study was the beginning of my becoming an individual separate from my family. I was focused on my peers and my social interactions with them. I did not really care that much about my ancestors or my parents' pasts. I was a typical early twenty something. When I told people I met about my family history, they seemed intrigued and very interested. The man I married did his doctoral dissertation on the differences in attitudes towards psychotherapy between Eastern European and German Jews, discovering that German Jews were more favorable to the concept, although few of my family members ever sought help from a psychotherapist.

One of the most important gifts my mother ever gave me was "permission" to leave home for college, making sure this happened for me, even while my father was against it. He felt it was wasteful to go away when there were perfectly good schools in the San Francisco area. I remain grateful today for my mother's insistence. The research on Holocaust survivors and their families supports the importance of socialization experiences outside of the small, insular family unit as one of the most important ways for the children of survivors to lead functional lives. Due to the many people I befriended and lived with, I began to see a much wider world.

I should also note that I always felt somewhat different from peers, though this did not prevent me from taking full opportunity of what college life offered. This is a common feeling among the offspring of immigrants and survivors of the Holocaust. The differences became more apparent to me during my adult years, as I compared myself to my adult friends, and began to see how differently I had been raised. My parents valued saving money, not being wasteful, and not following fads immediately. For example, we did not get a television until 1956. We only had one simple car and that we kept until it broke down. We did not have the newest gadgets or appliances. Another effect of growing up as a first-generation American is a tendency to fend more for oneself and learn independently about American customs and popular culture. Even though much social upheaval was occurring near me while I was growing up, I was not exposed to American popular culture, such as the Beatnik and folk music movement. I knew nothing about Beatnik culture and the famous artists that were only a few miles away from where I lived. I discovered The Weavers, the Seekers, Peter, Paul, and Mary, Pete Seeger, and Woody and Arlo Guthrie much later than most of my peers and learned to love this very American musical tradition at least ten years after they were well-known. However, I became a Beatles fan as soon as they appeared on the American scene in 1964, but that was teen culture to which I was exposed daily at school. And of course, the "Hippie" and anti-Vietnam War movement were definitely a part of my teen and young adult experience. I didn't need my parents to teach me about that!

Chapter 14

EVA

The years 1942-1945 were especially brutal for my mother and her fellow Jews. Not only were they living in deplorable conditions, with a lack of food, heat, and proper sanitation, they were also constantly threatened by the Japanese. However, my mother and her peers just persevered. What choice did they have really?

From 1944-45, my mother continued to work and play (to the extent possible) in Shanghai. In 1942-3, at 15, she met her first real boyfriend, described by my mother as "much older"— perhaps 21. It appears my mother was quite precocious in affairs of the heart, and, to this day, I believe she is popular with men. I presume she, and her peers, had quite the sense of adventure, though probably innocent by today's standards. I do know that he was popular, since I have seen references to him in books about the era. His name was Heinz Bergmann, known by his nickname, Pit. I know very little about him, other than that he was in Shanghai alone, as some German Jewish teenagers had left Germany without their parents, with the hope of reuniting after the war.

Eva and Pit, 1942-1944, approximately.

Reports of a German surrender made on May 10, 1945 was a joyous day for the Shanghailanders. However, the joy was exchanged with deep fear as the Shanghai Jews began to wonder about the fates of family and friends. As the allied forces liberated the concentration camps, stories began to circulate about the Nazi atrocities. My mother does not recount much about hearing these horrible tales, although the Wolffheim family had left behind two grandmothers, an aunt, an uncle and his family, and an uncle's wife.

Despite these ghastly revelations, there was celebration in the Jewish ghetto of Hongkew. However, at the same time, the first American bombers appeared over Shanghai, the beginning of yet more trauma for my mother and her fellow survivors. The Allied air forces had infiltrated the Japanese area of control, and my mother began to see B-17's, B-24's, and B-29's flying very low over the ghetto area, triggering the air raid sirens. In July, the Allied bombing of Shanghai began in earnest. Many of the Hongkew residents routinely slept on the roof to stay cool, my mother included, but now, not only did they worry about mosquitos, but also the situation raised the danger of the bombs. Mosquitos spread disease while bombs killed, so my mother has regaled us with stories of the inhabitants of her building moving inside, sitting under heavy dining room tables, with pots on their heads. Though the American pilots were not aiming for the Jews or the Chinese—they were after the Japanese Army—it was impossible in such a densely populated area to avoid collateral damage, as we now refer to deaths among innocent civilians. July 17, 1945 was the deadliest day, with 30 Jews and 500 Chinese killed. Based on military records, the bombing was fierce, dangerous, and sometimes deadly to the inhabitants. The risks were greater than the Hongkew residents realized, as there is evidence that the Japanese had military installations and munitions storage in the vicinity of the Jewish ghetto. A continuation of the war could have meant annihilation.

On August 7, 1945, word began to spread about the bombing of Hiroshima and Nagasaki, and a week later news flew around the ghetto lanes that Japan had surrendered. The war was finally over, and people were ecstatic.

The first American rescue mission arrived on August 18,

1945, and the American flag was substituted for the Japanese one. The first order of business was to release the P.O.W.'s and the civilians who had been interred. Then the United Nations Relief and Rehabilitation Administration (UNRAA) set up shop to assist the millions of Chinese who had lived under Japanese occupation. And the Jewish Distribution Committee (JDC) and Hebrew Immigrant Aid Society (HIAS) assisted the Jewish refugees. Army rations— luxuries to the deprived Europeans and Chinese—and medicines began to flow into Shanghai. My mother vividly describes her first view of the handsome, healthy, strong American soldiers, as they rode into the city in Jeeps. She began to taste American "delicacies", such as mayonnaise and Hershey's chocolate. At this time, the U.S. Army offered jobs to the American, British, and Chinese civilians. At a personal level for my mother, this was the best possible news and she soon found a job as a secretary to a U.S. Army officer.

Eva's boyfriend, Pit, learned around this time that the Nazis had murdered his entire family, and brokenhearted, he committed suicide. This must had been a terrible loss for my mother, as her father had died of cancer in the same year, 1946, and she had already lost a brother, uncle, girlfriend, and countless other acquaintances. My mother told me and my sister that she had a date to meet Pit at a bicycle shop. She was getting a new bicycle. He did not come which she reported as unusual behavior for him. However, later his friends found him in his apartment. I do not know the exact cause of death.

A note is in order about Ghoya, the sadistic Japanese official. After the Japanese surrender he returned to Shanghai for some reason. In a rare instance of violence by the Jews, he was attacked and finally fled. No one knows what happened to him. Some rumors have it that he was actually Korean and not Japanese. The memory of his face remains a nightmarish image for the Shanghailanders.

Chapter 15

KAREN

The term Holocaust began to be commonly heard in my young adult years. I remember that earlier I would hear that "6,000,000 Jews were killed", whispered in certain Jewish places—in the home, at religious school—but by the 70's and 80's, the subject was no longer discussed in hushed tones. I now knew that my parents' stories were part of this overall tragedy. Survivor was another new word that appeared. In 1978, the television miniseries, "Holocaust", was shown and, once more, I lived and breathed the story. I was already a young married woman at this time and I had read Leon Uris' book *QBVII*; Herman Wouk's books, *Winds of War* and *War and Remembrance*; and William Styron's, *Sophie's Choice*, to name a few books on the topic. My husband and I discussed these books at length and watched the mini-series together. I was stunned by these stories and for days walked around in a daze after watching a television mini-series or a movie in a theatre.

In the 1980's various books began to be written about the Jewish Shanghai experience, and I avidly read each book on the subject. The most well-known of these books is Ernest Heppner's *Shanghai Refuge*. My parents began to attend Shanghai Reunions

organized by newly formed groups of former refugees. These survivor organizations probably provided support and a sense of extended community for the former Shanghailanders and gave some
perspective to close-knit Holocaust survivor families like ours. My
mother renewed friendships. I felt a growing sense of positive
identity among this group of former refugees. The acceptance of a
Jewish or a specific immigrant identity in such close sympathetic
communities, as well as the absence of renewed, overt anti-Semitism, especially in the United States, may also have helped the survivors to become more comfortable and begin to speak of their experiences. She seemed happy to go to the reunions with her two
best friends, German Jewish refugees, who had also been émigrés
to Shanghai, along with my father and friends' spouses.

*Max and Eva
Levi, 1980's.*

In 1976 I married a Jewish man of Russian, Belorussian, and Latvian descent. His grandparents had come to the United States as very young children with their families or young adults to escape the pogroms carried out in the small towns and shetls of Eastern Europe. Plainly, we came from very different backgrounds. He came from a large, boisterous family. Yiddish phrases and jokes flew freely. For festive meals, they had huge amounts of typical Jewish food, for example bagels, lox, knishes, brisket, latkes, babka, tzimmes, to name a few. I had fun comparing these repasts to the more formal dinners, with definite courses, that I was used to. And no soda or catsup bottles on the table at my house! My family was small and more subdued. We were by no means fancy just more structured at meals. Our wedding reception was an interesting combination of Jewish dancing and folk songs, music from my generation, and the Big Band sound of my parents' time. It was a sit-down dinner with a rowdy component, definitely memorable. We met in Boston, and moved to the Washington, D.C. area to enable my husband to get a Ph.D. in Social Work. I have lived in the Maryland suburbs ever since. We adopted two children, Gabriel from Peru in 1990 and Isabel from Guatemala in 1993. We immersed ourselves and our children in their native cultures and learned as much as we could about Peru and Guatemala, visiting both countries on several occasions. While we also brought up our children to be Jewish, it is only in the last six or seven years that I have stressed this background to them.

In 2007, my sister and I joined my mother on a trip to China for her 80th birthday. When we went to Shanghai, we visited Hong Kou, the new name for Hongkew. We found a guide and he joined us as my mother found her way to her old building on Tongshan Road.

The three of us looked up at the veranda and we tried to peek in the windows. The structure was in dismal condition but it was standing.

Eva at 3 Tongshan Road, 2007.

A group of women, who were my mother's age, came out and we told them our story in abbreviated form, with the help of the guide. A picture was taken. There was not much else for her to show us, for most of Hong Kou had been rebuilt. We went down a few familiar streets and went to a few green areas. We stopped at two plaques commemorating the Jewish ghetto. We passed a large, low brick building. My mother pointed it out, and said, "That was the Ward Street Jail. That is where we ran during the bombing. We knew the Americans would not bomb the building that held the Allied POW's."

Ward Street Jail.

She showed us Chusan Road, the "Broadway" of the ghetto, also known as "Little Vienna", for all of the European style stores and cafes that existed during the 1930's and 1940's.

I visited Israel in 1973 and in 2013. Both of these trips were powerful experiences in different ways. I feel a deep emotional attachment to the land and the people. The first trip was a typical young person's trip. I visited all of the usual sights and I hung out with other people my age from all over the world. We went on strenuous excursions to the Galilee, the Dead Sea, and Masada. In 2013, I took an unusual trip with my present congregation, Bethesda Jewish Congregation in Bethesda, Maryland. The trip was a dual narrative, during which we learned about the Israeli—Palestinian conflict from both sides. We visited people and places in Israel and in Palestine, and we heard different stories from various perspectives. It was quite enlightening and deepened my understanding of recent conflicts and the region overall. My cousin Ralph Salinger took me around northern Israel and we ended our tour at Degania. He took me to an old tank and showed me where the battle for this kibbutz took place. Furthermore, he told me that one of my relatives died at this spot, defending her kibbutz and her land in the War of Independence in 1948. I felt very proud that a hero's blood ran through me. I also met with Alon Liel, who along with his brother are my second cousins. (I do not have first cousins.) Alon was a diplomat, but now he is working tirelessly for peace. His wife heads an organization that helps underprivileged individuals in Israel.

The Olympic Games have fascinated my mother, since she first experienced them in 1936. Our family visited the site of the 1960 Winter Games in Squaw Valley, a few months after the actual competitions, for a spring snow trip. The first actual games my mother attended were the 1984 Summer Olympics in Los Angeles. Even though she was uncomfortable in crowds, she went to several events. Her love of the event overrode her distaste for large groups of people congregating for a particular purpose. My mother invited all of us—my father, brother, sister and me—for a family reunion in Los Angeles. My brother and my mother also attended the 1996 Summer Olympic Games in Atlanta, Georgia. I believe the pride she felt when Jesse Owens won his medal and angered Hitler has remained strong over the years and she celebrates every time the Olympics occurs. She continues to watch the games on television.

The ambivalence my parents demonstrated about their heritage resulted in my own conflicted feelings, for many years. When I was a college student, the question was should I continue to study German or choose another major? When I traveled to Europe in 1973, the pressing concern was should I separate from my traveling partner and make a visit to Germany or skip the country as most Jews were doing? Later on, as I matured, the problem was do I hate Germany and Germans or do I realize that the Germans alive are not guilty of atrocities? And most recently, do I embrace the German part of my heritage or disown it? I began to think about the good years my ancestors spent in Germany, thriving economically and socially. What about the achievements Jewish and Christian Austrians and Germans have made, especially in the mid-19th century to early 20th century? And most personally, do I disconnect with those very personal memories of my grandmothers and their very German qualities? All contemporary Jews struggle with these questions; however, they are poignant concerns to German Jews and their offspring. In my discussions with others, I have found the most negative and narrow-minded feelings towards Germany and Germans among Jews who are not of German descent. I suppose these Jews do not feel the pressing need to reconcile their German ancestry with their Jewish heritage.

After an interaction with my cousin Ralph Salinger, in Israel, when he pointed out my very "Prussian" qualities of being precise, organized, timely, I realized that I might not even have a choice in this question. Nonetheless, I determined that I did not want to change these qualities in me. I am now comfortable with being German Jewish and do not hesitate to be proud of the achievements German Jews made over the centuries. I have two

German friends, and we speak fondly of German traditions. And I do so, without connecting these foods and practices with Nazis. The fact of the matter is that my two friends loathe the Nazis as much as I do.

In 2014, I planned a trip to Central Europe. I met my mother in Berlin. We spent a week there, and we visited her old house, site of a school and synagogue, and several museums and memorials which brought back the past. We walked from her house through the park to the zoo and then to a fashionable downtown area.

Plaque by Hotel Kempinski in Berlin, stating that this was a hotel owned by Jews, was taken from them by the Nazis and "returned" in

1952. The plaque states that this history should not be forgotten.

I saw where she went as a child with her family and friends and heard stories as we walked. The city brought back many anecdotes, which she did share. It was a fantastic experience. We rode the subways, as she had, and I heard more stories. With a friend, we traveled outside the city to Wannsee, where she had swam as a child. This is also the site of the Wannsee Conference, during which the Nazis set down the plans for the "Final Solution" for Jews and other undesirables, as the Nazis referred to Communists, Gypsies, people with special needs, and homosexuals. I was also aware that Berlin and its surrounding suburbs was a place of horrible events, from the Nazis through the Communist era. Standing by the remnants of the Wall that separated East and West Berlin was a stark reminder of the myriad horrors that had occurred. I could almost hear the sound of screams and shouts and gunfire. Sometimes, we just had fun—a boat ride down the Spree River and shopping at the beautiful department store KDW (Kaufhaus des Westens), which has not changed in its overall purpose since the 1930's. And, of course, we ate sausages, drank beer, and had "iced coffee" which is a delightful concoction of coffee, ice cream, and whipped cream.

It was not until 2014 that I finally reconciled my feelings about Germans and Germany. I hate what happened; however, I no longer abhor Germany and its people. I recognize the amends the people have made regarding the atrocities of the Holocaust. I have spoken to Germans who are my age and they feel, much as I do, that the murder of millions of people is incomprehensible. I have stepped on the Stolperstein and visited the memorials in Berlin. I have read about the suffering of the non-Jewish Germans during and after World War II.

Chapter 16

EVA

In the spring of 1946, there was more suffering and death for my mother and grandmother. Karl, my grandfather, Eva's father, and Kaethe's husband, died of cancer, after a great deal of pain and misery. The treatment of cancer was in its infancy in 1946 and primitive at best, by our standards. Obviously, a hospital in Shanghai could not have had the best equipment and facilities just one year after the end of the war. Although my grandmother was a nurse, she must have felt powerless to lessen my grandfather's suffering. Of course, this added to the heartaches my mother and grandmother would bring to America. Uncles Eugen, Gunther and Grandfather Karl were buried in one of the several Jewish cemeteries in Shanghai, but, tragically, they have all been bulldozed over with high-rise apartments built on this sacred ground.

In the summer of 1946, Eva and Kaethe were waiting for their turn to leave China. My mother reported that she was desperate and depressed at this stage. She said that she "left her mother alone" in Shanghai and went to Nanking (Nanjing) to work for the U.S. Army. My mother told this part of her narrative to my sister and me during a visit to Shanghai in 2007. She admits that she "regrets" her decision to leave and that she "knew her mother was suffering from grief". My mother was 19 and had already had a lifetime of experiences. She went north to another Chinese city, along with many other young Jews, to live and work and play among the Americans and other foreigners. She was in Nanking one year; but it was a busy time, with many social events, work, and attention from various male suitors. On my most recent trip to San Francisco in August 2015, my mother pulled out a photo album, heretofore unknown to my sister and me. She showed us pictures of herself with various female and male friends.

Of course, these youngsters were completely enamored of the American G.I.'s in their nifty uniforms and well-stocked PX's. Her friend, Ruth, even fell in love with one and married him. This was Forrest Sumner, a handsome, rugged Floridian, who I came to know during my childhood. It was in Nanking, that my mother learned American English, including slang, and ate mess hall food (which was nutritious and delicious after years of near starvation).

Mayonnaise and butter have significant meaning in my mother's life. My mother never really had mayonnaise as a child. One day, her friend Ruth's fiancée, Forrest, brought a jar of mayonnaise as a treat. The two young women, Eva and Ruth, feasted on mayonnaise sandwiches with pickles. They just couldn't get enough of the creamy white spread. Their bodies were obviously deprived of fat. Even today, mayonnaise is my mother's choice for sandwiches over mustard. Butter, of course, was a mainstay of the German diet, used in cooking and as the most common spread put on bread. The refugees in China could not get much butter or any other fat for that matter, and, probably as a consequence, my mother retains an insatiable appetite for butter. My mother recounts that she and her compatriots were fat-deprived, telling me that they used to eat fried pork fat and rinds on bread, during the war, just to get some fat.

Ruth and Eva, 2015, the mayonnaise-eating partners.

My mother has painted a picture of her Nanking stay as light, bright, and lively. There was a group of young, energetic Jews who transferred to Nanking temporarily for a change of pace and an opportunity to earn more money and to stay occupied. They worked hard and played hard. The shadow of death and loss must have been very close among both Europeans and Chinese. The horrible news from Europe was still fresh in people's minds and most Jews were still searching for missing loved ones. Nanking had been the site of a terrible massacre by the Japanese in 1937. These teenagers and young adults were still determined to live life to the fullest. My mother made an entirely new set of friends in Nanking, some of whom she remained in contact with long after the war years ended.

Eva, relaxing and flirting in Nanking (Nanging).

Back in Shanghai, the American Consulate had opened and was processing Jews for immigration to the United States. There was a quota again, and there was constant fear that they wouldn't be able to finally go to America.

The Johnson Act of 1924 established quotas for immigrants based on country of origin and was created due to insecurities arising out of World War I. The problem now was that there was no provision for the hundreds of thousands of displaced persons from World War II. As a result, President Harry Truman issued an executive directive in late 1945 that increased immigration quotas for persons displaced by the Nazi regime. Under this order, of the more than 41,000 displaced persons who immigrated to the United States, approximately 28,000 were Jews. In 1948, the US Congress passed the Displaced Persons Act, which provided for another 400,000 displaced persons to enter the United States between January 1, 1949, and December 31, 1952.

In Shanghai, each family received a number at the Consulate and another wait began, though some Jews decided to go to Palestine, Australia, and New Zealand. My mother wanted to go to the United States, most probably because of her exposure to the Americans in Nanking and, in addition, my mother's family members were not Zionists, so Palestine probably wouldn't have been a first choice.

My mother and grandmother had to wait an entire year before sailing out of the harbor of Shanghai in the fall of 1947. They were the first to leave their building. When the families emigrated from Shanghai at the end of the war, the remaining families bought out the family that left. The last family to leave sold the building and contents to a Chinese policeman, but they never actually received the money from the sale. My mother and grandmother must have received visas based on the executive directive that Truman made in 1945, but it is difficult to know, since the issuing of visas has always been a murky business.

Flat on Tongshan Road, as seen in 2007.

The ship made its first stop in Hong Kong and, evidently, my mother knew a man who worked in a hotel, a friend of a friend, with whom she spent the day touring Hong Kong. I imagine my grandmother must have been sick with worry at her absence. Later, my mother was ill on the ship and had to be quarantined, creating more trouble and worry for the mother and daughter. Eva was no longer the carefree, frolicking child who had enjoyed an adventure on a slow boat to China. They also stopped in Honolulu, which was probably their first exposure to a new way of life. Then, on to California, sailing through the Golden Gate of San Francisco in late December of 1947. My mother and her mother stood on the deck and watched the ship go through the famous Golden Gates. Of course, my mother does not remember the weather, but I imagine bright blue cloudless skies and a crisp, brisk wind blowing as the large ship made its way under the majestic bridge and on toward the Embarcadero, the wharf area near the Ferry Building at the San Francisco Bay.

It had been a lifetime within a lifetime, since they had left

Hamburg, Germany on another large ship. Their small family had been reduced by half. Now there were only two single women, one young and one in her mid-fifties, both intelligent, strong, but traumatized.

The JDC first sent my mother and grandmother to Fresno, California. According to my mother, the standard operating procedure in the late 40's was to disperse Jewish refugees all over the United States, not just on "the coasts". My mother and her mother lived in Fresno, a small, quiet Central Valley town, for one year. My mother has told us that the Jewish community in Fresno welcomed them warmly and they made friends, describing warm, gentle evenings and kind people. My mother had a good job with a Jewish doctor, honing her skills as a laboratory technologist.

Eva and Kaethe (center) in Fresno, California, 1948.

But Eva and Kaethe were big city people and a year later, in December 1948, they moved to San Francisco, where my mother has lived since. They found a small apartment, and Eva again went to work in a hospital lab, drawing and analyzing blood taken from patients. She began her studies in earnest to receive her California License for Laboratory Technicians. Again, she was lucky to find doctors who were willing to help her learn the field. My grandmother also immediately made new friends and found work as a Practical Nurse, what we would now call a Home Health Aide. Apparently, neither spent time thinking about the past. They moved on to a better future.

Eva also went to night school and received her General Equivalency Degree (GED) and years later, in May 2000, she was the oldest graduate of San Francisco State University for that class, receiving a Bachelor of Arts in Liberal Arts.

Epilogue

"The awareness of one's origins is like an anchor line plunged into the deep, keeping one within a certain range. Without it, historical intuition is virtually impossible."
- *Milosz*, Native Realm

For me, modern history has been made real by listening to and retelling personal stories, both those of my family and of others. I can feel the pain and the implications of virulent anti-Semitism when I think about my mother as a small child being told she couldn't play in certain places or with Christian children or go to familiar shops. I feel the tragedy of war when I think about my grandmother and her mother (my Great Grandmother Rosa) suffering forever with the loss of two young brothers/sons in World War I. I can feel fear when I think about a middle-aged couple (my Grandparents Karl and Kaethe) having to forgo their comfortable life—actually have treasured belongings and a way of life stolen by thugs—venturing to a primitive and mysterious place (China). As I sit on my deck on a muggy Maryland morning, I feel the oppressive, unending heat of a Shanghai summer in pre-air conditioning times. When my fingers start to hurt from holding a leash or shoveling snow on a cold January afternoon, I think of Jewish women and men moving heavy stones in concentration and labor camps, literally under a Nazi gun. I think of being sick and afraid, on and off, for nine years, in a rat-infested neighborhood and be-ing taken to primitive, frightening hospitals where more people died than lived. I try to remember how these experiences can shape a person forever and also influence the next generation and maybe even future generations.

My mother has always been a collection of contradictions; quiet and withholding and also opinionated and emphatic; and loving "the finer things in life" yet continuously denying herself. What she has not been ambiguous about is her keenness to live in the present, not the past. Certainly living day-by-day and "in the moment" has been shown to be advisable as opposed to chronically allowing one's mind to wander and ponder the past or the future. It is important to be mindful of the present; the pre-sent is all we ever really have and the next present and so on. However, learning about the past can clarify the present and im-prove the future, as I have humbly attempted to elucidate in these pages.

I am not without flaws, and I certainly continue to get frus-trated when my mother exhibits quirky behavior. I have visited undeveloped countries and stepped over raw sewage. It is diffi-cult to imagine living in these circumstances for nine years; the smell alone is horrendous. It is important to mention my mother's fear of germs and dirt on clothing and food. With no dis-respect intended, my sister and I could regale anyone with stories of how my mother washes clothes and dishes. My mother is not really afraid of much, especially becoming ill, but she scrubs out clothes and silverware with a vengeance to this day, although she no longer needs to do so. While we have tried to get her to stop this almost-neurotic behavior, the power of a traumatic past can have an effect on a person's daily actions and personality for years afterward. "For heaven's sake," I say, "Take the taxi, get the nicer coat, go to a luxury hotel, and get your nails done." But my mother just can't get herself to do these things, unless we siblings lead her by the hand. Children like my siblings and I assume the role of being parents to our own parents. In discussing the relationships between Survivors and their children, Helen Motro (1996) explains: "We are older now than our parents were when they survived. And yet they in their old age still feel like orphans, and we often feel like their parents. It is our duty to fill all voids."

Karen and Eva, 2015, Selfie.

I want our children to know the past, so it is not repeated. Being aware of history enables new generations to gain a greater understanding of human nature and what can come to pass. Knowledge of the past is a lifeline to what was and what will be. For example, if my son knows that genocide happened in Germany, he will be more aware of the violence people can commit and be a wiser and proactive citizen. I want my children to respect their elders, for certainly older people have worked hard to gain respect, and many values that guided their lives should not be lost. I hope my children, and nieces and nephews will know something of their grandparents and great grandparents' lives, as those lives are anchors for them as well as for me. As a responsible parent, I have tried to put a halt to the old behaviors that were necessary for survival without forgetting to instill the all-important values of perseverance, hard work, some degree of thriftiness, and education. This is a difficult task. For it is easy to throw off old dysfunctional behaviors; but, it is not so easy to remember the worthwhile values hidden in the old ways.

Now that I am in my sixth decade and my mother is in her eighth, I have come to be more understanding and tolerant of my mother's ways. She is not telling me everything she remembers about Berlin or Shanghai, but that is not necessary. I respect her privacy, but I do feel the fool when I share some Shanghai discovery with her only to have her say, "Oh that, didn't you know? Of course, so and so...." She has either forgotten what she has told me or knows very well she never divulged that story. It sometimes seems that she wants me to find information and then she can behave as if it was obvious all along. Or she has a bit of the rascal in her, feeling that if I want to have details about her past, I should seek out the information on my own, or perhaps my exploration jiggles her memories loose.

Certainly, as is evident from this story, Eva has had the love of at least two men and many close friends and that of her family, including her parents and children and mother-in-law. She has had tremendous good luck in health and longevity and intelligence. She was also blessed with the luck of avoiding death from disease and the consequences of war, both in Europe and Asia. However, I believe that it is her tenacious character that has brought her through life. Eva is stubborn, strong, and optimistic. And she never relinquishes her dreams until they are fulfilled.

Eva reluctantly using 21st century technology

I often feel unwise when talking to my mother; she likes to be the "devil's advocate", and she is very good at the role. She is a smart lady and can discuss her side forever with well-developed and sound arguments and not give an inch. We also disagree a great deal. We are both products of our times. I am accustomed to these dynamics now and have developed a thicker skin. I am not as easily hurt as I used to be when talking to my mother or asking her questions.

To further illustrate my mother's continuing ambivalence concerning the exploration of her early life, my sister recently told me the story of the former "den" or family room. I have attempted to enter this room several times. My mother has been accumulating old mail and phone books, pictures, and other yet identified stuff. She has closed off the room, since my father died, which means no one is allowed in, except her. Entering the room creates the risk of getting yelled at by my mother, not to mention being assaulted by dust, mold and allergens. What is in there? I don't believe there is any shocking information concealed in the room, just an accumulation of items and communications from friends and family members. Occasionally, my mother will send me a tidbit. My sister quietly entered the room not long ago, borrowing some pictures at my request. The poor quality of the photographs attests to the dismal conditions in which they are stored. Everything is slowly deteriorating in the dark, musty, and ever-moist San Francisco environment. This is how my mother chooses to cope with and store her memories, happy and sad, proud and tragic. My siblings and I may not understand this behavior; however, it is my mother's privilege to save and keep information as she wishes.

My mother is now identifying me as the keeper of the family history and not with the disdain of past years. She has even praised my reading, writing, photography, and sense of humor. Furthermore, she is beginning to admire my steadfast nature and self-discipline and to respect some of the difficult choices I have had to make in my life. I think I am finally gaining her admiration. I just regret that it has taken so long. However, I have had to earn her esteem, which makes perfect sense to me now. I had to work hard and demonstrate to my mother that I was worthy of respect. And that is how it should be.

In conclusion, I have been very excited to learn about my relatives through my mother's stories and with help from various relatives. I thought my Berlin relations were staid upper middle class businessmen and their sophisticated, cultured wives. I have come to learn that many of my relatives were risk takers and heroes. Rosa and Hugo Warschauer moved from a small town in Prussia to Berlin for more business opportunities. My grandmother Kaethe was a nurse in World War I; her brothers lost their lives in World War I. My grandfathers were soldiers in the trenches of the Great War, fighting for Germany. Klara Wolffheim, my paternal great grandmother, opened a clothing store, which her daughter Emmy subsequently ran. Klara's son, Eugen, my great uncle, went to America with his wife and tried out life in the United States, in the early part of the 20th century. He managed his wife who had a vaudeville act. Some of my grandmother's aunts and cousins went to Palestine, prior to independence, and helped settle a new country. My mother's Uncle Albert was a ship's captain, which was definitely an adventurous career.

Addendum

A short history of Shanghai and its European residents during the colonial and postcolonial period is in order. Trade between China and Europe began with silks, porcelain and tea. To offset the financial trade shortfalls caused by the intense public demand for tea, the British began to ship opium from colonial India to China during the 18th and 19th centuries. Opium addiction in China intensified and in 1729 had become such a problem that the emperor outlawed the sale and smoking of opium. That action did not decrease the trade, and in 1796 the emperor forbade opium importation and cultivation. Nevertheless, the opium trade continued to flourish. The Qing Dynasty (1644-1911) continued to try to halt the spread of opium by seizing opium supplies from British traders. This resulted in the First Opium War fought between China and Britain from 1839 to 1842, which the British won. As a result, five ports in China were opened up to Britain. They were Shanghai, Ningpo (Ningbo), Fuzhow (Fuzhou), Amoy (Xian), and Canton (Guangzhou). Hong Kong was ceded outright to the British. Soon after, the British, Americans, and French arrived to do business and live in China. The International Settlement of Shanghai was established in 1854 when British, French, and American consuls divided the city into concessions or settlements, establishing the French and International Settlements or Concessions of Shanghai. The latter consisted of American and British areas and were governed by the Shanghai Municipal Council. The French Concession, ruled by the French, took in many émigrés between 1900-1914; following World War I and the Bolshevik Revolution, many so-called White Russians (as opposed to Red, or Communist, Russians) escaped to China and lived in the French Concession. After the Japanese invaded Manchuria in 1931, more refugees spilled into Shanghai. The Japanese attacked Chinese troops in Shanghai in 1932, thereby violating a treaty of neutrality. British, French and American troops came to Shanghai to support the Chinese. The Japanese gradually gained influence in the city, by purchasing businesses and attempting to gain favor with resident westerners (non-Asians) and finally invading Shanghai in 1937. This act of aggression started the second Sino-Japanese War. The Japanese were the superior force and eventually "won" the conflict; however, the Chinese mounted a determined resistance, and there were many casualties on both sides. The war lasted three months. After the conflict, the Japanese took over governing the International Settlement.

二战期间犹太难民居住区

第二次世界大战期间，数万犹太人为逃避法西斯的迫害来到上海。日本侵华当局以犹太难民"无国籍"为由设立隔离区，对他们的行动加以限制。此区域西起公平路，东至通北路，南起惠民路，北至周家嘴路。

虹口区人民政府

THE DESIGNATED AREA FOR STATELESS REFUGEES

From 1937 to 1941, thousands of Jews came to Shanghai fleeing from Nazi persecution. Japanese occupation authorities regarded them as "stateless refugees" and set up this designated area to restrict their residence and business. The designated area was bordered on the west by Gongping Road, on the east by Tongbei Road, on the south by Huimin Road, and on the north by Zhoujiazui Road.

Hongkou District People's Government

מצבה לזכר תושבי השכונה היהודים בתקופת מלחמת העולם השנייה

משנת 1937 ועד שנת 1941 הגיעו לשנגחאי כעשרים אלף יהודים שנמלטו מהצורר הנאצי ומצאו בה מקלט הפליטים היהודים אותם הגדיר שלטון הכיבוש היפני "חסרי נתינותי" יהורה להם להתגורר

A plaque we found in Hong Kou, 2007.

Acknowledgments

I wanted to write a book about my mother for many years. At first, it was just a fantasy or pipe dream. Then, life got in the way, and I was just too busy raising children and working. When I retired, friends said, "Now, you can write that book". But still I did not start. Then, my sister became ill and I realized that I did not have unlimited time on this earth. In the summer of 2014, I took a trip to Berlin with my mother. After I returned, I started writing. I took the advice of a writer I once met. She said, "Write. Everyone has a story."

The first catalyst was the family tree that my cousin, Ralph Salinger, created in the 1980's. I devoured every book that was written about Shanghai, China, and World War II. Then came the trip to China in 2007. In May 2013, I visited Ralph in Israel. His infectious curiosity and diligence spurred me on to write my story.

I would like to thank my editor, JoMarie Acosta, for her intelligence, kindness and critical analysis. Without her, I would have a glorified Social Studies Report. Thomas Peterson is a new email friend, who provided a great deal of interesting information regarding Eugen and Elspeth Wolffheim. Fred Cohn was generous with his information and photographs. I acknowledge all of the Shangailanders, who over the years provided me with rich information, knowingly or unknowingly. Some are Inge Rosenthal, Ruth Sumner, Anita Schaie. I am thankful for my grandmother,

Omi Kaethe, who was funny, generous, and troubled. She was the mother, who had to sacrifice so much, on her path of survival to a better place, San Francisco. Of course, I must thank my sister, Connie Levi, for her never ending love and support. Without her, life would be lonely and not as pleasant. And last but not least, the heroine of this tale, my mother, Eva Levi. She is brave and strong and stubborn and has survived.

Bibliography

Allsop, Amelia. "The Lost Records Revealed: Hong Kong Heritage
   Project's Jewish Collection". *Asian Jewish Life*.
   http://asianjewishlife.org/pages/articles/winter2010-
   11/AJL_Feature_TheLostRecords.html

"Anti-Jewish Decrees". *Learning Voices of the Holocaust*. British
   Library. http://www.bl.uk/learning/histciti-
   zen/voices/info/decrees/decrees.html

Avison, William, Jane D. McLeod, and Bernice A. Pescosolido,
   eds. *Mental Health, Social Mirror*. New York: Springer Science and Business Media, 2007. pp. 174-75.

Bacon, Ursula. *Shanghai Diary*. Milwaukie, Oregon: Milestone
   Press, 2002.

Blumenthal, W. Michael. *From Exile to Washington*. New York:
   Overlook Press, 2013

Burston, Bradley. "The 'Exodus' Effect: The Monumentally Fic-
   tional Israel That Remade American Jewry. *Haaretz*. 9 Jan.
   2012. http://www.haaretz.com/weekend/week-s-end/the-
   exodus-effect-the-monumentally-fictional-israel-that-re-
   made-american-jewry-1.476411

Chang, Wayne. "Ho Feng Shan: The 'Chinese Schindler' who saved thousands of Jews". *CNN*. 24 Jul. 2015. http://www.cnn.com/2015/07/19/asia/china-jews-schindler-ho-feng-shan/

Davis, Becky. "Ancient Chinese Community Celebrates Its Jewish Roots, and Passover". *The New York Times*. Sinosphere: Dispatches From China. 6 Apr. 2015. http://sinosphere.blogs.nytimes.com/2015/04/06/kaifeng-china-jewish-roots-passover/?smid=fb-share

Eber, Irene. *Wartime Shanghai and the Jewish Refugees from Central Europe: Survival, Co-Existence, and Identity in a Multi-Ethnic City*. Berlin, Germany: de Gruyter, 2012.

Elgin, Duane and Coleen LeDrew Elgin. *Living Legacies*. Berkeley, Californica: Canari Press, 2001. p. 17.

Elon, Amos. *The Pity of it All*. New York: Picador, 2002.

Goldsmith, Martin. *The Inextinguishable Symphony*. New York: John Wiley and Sons, 2000.

Guesnet, François. "East Prussia". *YIVO Institute for Jewish Research*. The YIVO Encyclopedia of Jews in Eastern Europe. Translated by Deborah Cohen. http://www.yivoencyclopedia.org/article.aspx/East_Prussia

Guesnet, François. "Kaliningrad". *YIVO Institute for Jewish Research*. The YIVO Encyclopedia of Jews in Eastern Europe. Translated by Deborah Cohen. http://www.yivoencyclopedia.org/article.aspx/Kaliningrad

Hackett, Bob and Sander Kingsepp. "The Seizure of Shanghai's International Settlement – 1941". *Imperial Japanese Navy Page.* Rising Storm – The Imperial Japanese Navy and China 1931-1941. http://www.combinedfleet.com/International_t.htm

Hampl, Patricia. *I Could Tell You Stories: Sojourns in the Land of Memory.* New York: Norton & Company, 1999.

Heppner, Ernest G. *Shanghai Refuge: A Memoir of the World War II Jewish Ghetto.* Lincoln, Nebraska: University of Nebraska Press, 1995.

"Immigration Act of 1924 (The Johnson-Reed Act), The". *U.S. Department of State.* Office of the Historian. https://history.state.gov/milestones/1921-1936/immigration-act

Isherwood, Christopher. *The Berlin Stories.* 1963. Reprint. New York: New Directions, 2008.

Kaplan, Marion A. *Between Dignity and Despair.* New York: Oxford University Press, 1996.

Kellermann, Natan P. F., PhD. "Transmission of Holocaust Trauma". AMCHA – National Israeli Center for Psychosocial Support of Survivors of the Holocaust and the Second Generation. https://yadvashem.org/yv/en/education/languages/dutch/pdf/kellermann.pdf

Kolbert, Elizabeth. "The Last Trial: A great-grandmother, Auschwitz, and the arc of justice". *The New Yorker.* 16 Feb. 2015. http://www.newyorker.com/magazine/2015/02/16/last-trial

McDonald, James G. *To the Gates of Jerusalem: The Diaries and Papers of James G. McDonald, 1945-1947*. Edited by Norman J.W. Goda, Barbara McDonald Stewart, Severin Hochberg, and Richard Breitman. Bloomington, Indiana: Indiana University Press, 2014

Mowrer, Edgar Ansel. *Germany Puts The Clock Back*. London, UK: John Lane The Bodley Head Limited, 1933.

"Museum History". *Asian Art Museum*. http://www.asianart.org/about/history

"Opium Trade". *Encyclopedia Britannica*. British and Chinese History. http://www.britannica.com/EB-checked/topic/430160/opium-trade

Pietsch, Jani. *Ich besass einen Garten in Schoneiche bei Berlin*. Frankfurt, Germany: Campus Verlag, 2006. pp. 52-56.

Rich, Tracey R. "Yiddish Language and Culture". *Judaism 101*. www.jewfaq.org/yiddish.htm

Shulevitz, Judith. "The Science of Suffering". *New Republic*. 16 Nov. 2014. http://www.newrepublic.com/article/120144/trauma-genetic-scientists-say-parents-are-passing-ptsd-kids

Swiggum, S. and M. Kohli. "German East Africa Line / Woermann Line". *TheShipsList*. www.theshipslist.com/ships/lines/woermann.shtml

Tokayer, Marvin and Mary Swartz. *The Fugu Plan: The Untold Story of the Japanese and the Jews During World War II.* 1979. Reprint. Jerusalem, Israel: Gefen Publishing House, 2004.

Tugend, Tom. "'Jewish Refugees in Shanghai' tells story of survival". *Jewish Journal.* 16 Oct. 2013. http://www.jewishjournal.com/culture/article/jewish_refugees_in_shanghai_tells_story_of_survival

Valent, Paul. "Transgenerational Transmission of Grief; Using the Holocaust as an Example". Nalag Conference. 20 Oct. 1999. http://www.paulvalent.com/wp-content/uploads/2013/02/loss_death_grief_07.pdf

Vámos, Péter. "'Home Afar': The Life of Central European Jewish Refugees in Shanghai During World War II". *Acta Orientalia* 57.1 (2004): 55-70.

Wawrzyn, Heidemarie. "Wormditt". *Destroyed German Synagogues and Communities.* http://germansynagogues.com/index.php/synagogues-and-communities?pid=71&sid=1379:wormditt

Wilson, John P., Zev Harel, and Boaz Kahana, eds. *Human Adaptation to Extreme Stress: From the Holocaust to Vietnam.* New York: Plenum Press, 1988. pp. 199-200.

Index

Made in the USA
Middletown, DE
13 February 2020